Motocross Racers

30 Years of Legendary Dirt Bikes

Ray Ryan

*Photography by Bill Forsyth
and Jeremy Holland*

MOTORBOOKS

This edition first published in 2003 by Motorbooks International, an imprint of MBI Publishing Company, Galtier Plaza, Suite 200, 380 Jackson Street, St. Paul, MN 55101-3885 USA

Motorbooks International titles are also available at discounts in bulk quantity for industrial or sales-promotional use. For details write to Special Sales Manager at Motorbooks International Wholesalers & Distributors, Galtier Plaza, Suite 200, 380 Jackson Street, St. Paul, MN 55101-3885 USA.

Library of Congress Cataloging-in-Publication Data

Ryan, Ray, 1948-
    Motorcross racers / by Rya Ryan.
        p. cm.
    ISBN 0-7603-1239-7 (pbk. : alk. paper)
    1. Motocross. 2. Motorcycles, Racing. I. Title.

GV1060.12.R93 2003
796. 7'56—dc21

On the front cover: This 1978 RC500 competed in the World Championship with Brad Lackey aboard. *Bill Forsyth*

On the frontispiece: The engine of a 1974 CCM Works Replica. *Jim Godo*

On the title page: A Les Archer Norton Manx. *Bill Forsyth*

On the back cover, left: This 1979 Yamaha HL500 was custom-built using a YZ frame and a TT500 motor. Dry weight was amazingly close to that of modern open-classers. *Bill Forsyth*. **Right:** This 1974 Suzuki RH250 is in action vintage racing in 2000. *Bill Forsyth*

Editor: Lee Klancher
Designer: LeAnn Kuhlmann

Printed in China

Contents

Acknowledgments

I wish to thank the many friends, motocross champions, and motorcycle industry people who have assisted in the research and production of *Motocross Racers*. For background knowledge and information, I thank Hans Appelgren, Geoff Ballard, Steve Bysouth, Peter Drakeford, Mark Firkin, Andrew George, Clem Nunn, Jim Scaysbrook, and Ken Smith (Australia); Jiri Starec (Czech Republic); Simon Cheney and Pat French (England); Francois Stauffacher (Spain); Mikael Saksi, Nisse Wedin, and Ake Wremp (Sweden); Norm Bigelow, Paul Stannard, Reese Dengler, Mark Thompson, and Craig Comontofski (U.S.A.).

I also wish to thank the many motorcycle owners for their contributions, including Neil Baker, Gary Benn, Darren Cheney, Rick Cotton, Tony McMahon, Fred Robins, Dave Tanner, Rob Twyerould of the Motorex KTM Team, Bob Voumard, and Brian Watson (Australia); Lee Fabry, Jim Godo, Terry Good, Jeff Hill, Pat Knopp, John LeFevre, Maico Moe, Fred Mork, Bob and Linda Neilson, Kelly Owen, Michael Tillman, Mike Tolle, and Tom White (U.S.A.).

For the ongoing history lessons, I acknowledge and thank Stephen Gall, Jeff Leisk, and Trevor Williams (Australia); Harry Everts (Belgium); Jaroslav Falta (Czech Republic); Alan Clews (England); Les Archer (Spain); Torsten Hallman and Hakan Andersson (Sweden); Roger DeCoster, Tom Halverson, Brad Lackey, Jim Pomeroy, and Jeff Smith (U.S.A.); as well as some who prefer to remain anonymous.

I am also indebted to photographers Phil England and Geoff Morris (Australia); Nick Haskell and Chris Malam (England); Ake Wremp (Sweden); Mitch Friedman and Dorian Sleeper (U.S.A).

My partner, Barbara Cash, also deserves a long overdue "Thank you" for living with phone calls in the middle of the night!

—Ray Ryan
Perth, Western Australia

Introduction

From the 1960s to today, motocross has created its own heroes, legends, and icons. The motorcycles that punctuate the sport are diverse and individual. Some are now synonymous with the champions who raced them, while others have earned their immortality by etching themselves in the hearts and minds of ordinary racers who rode in the dirt to pursue their personal dreams.

These bikes range from slender chrome-and-alloy British thumpers to featherweight European and Japanese two-strokes. Others are hardcore form-follows-function factory weapons, built solely for winning in the arena of Grand Prix motocross.

Each motorcycle in *Motocross Racers* deserves a permanent place in the culture of motocross. Because this is not a history book, our selection criteria were broader than simply the number of races a bike may have won. Our goal was to document the evolution of motocross through key machines that define the timelines of the sport—that highlight the evolution of motocross from amateur to professional and its expansion from European to international in under 50 years. We also chose certain bikes because they reflect changes beyond the nuts and bolts of motorcycle design. In their day, they characterized an emerging new motocross subculture that influenced the social attitudes, the fashions, and even the daily dialogue of young people from San Francisco, California, to Sydney, Australia.

—Ray Ryan, *author*
Bill Forsyth, *photographer*
Jeremy Holland, *photographer*

PART 1

The 1960s

The Les Archer Manx Norton 500

The Last Legend

A DOHC cylinder head was teamed with a compact Mahle hard-chrome barrel, twin-plug ignition, and around 11:1 compression. *Bill Forsyth*

Fitted with a DOHC short-stroke Manx Norton motor, this final evolution of the Manx Norton motocrossers raced by Les Archer throughout the fifties and sixties is a tactile monument to ingenuity and raw power.

Englishman Les Archer was a second-generation motorcycle racer, following in the Archer family tradition of his road-racer father, Leslie, who was nicknamed "The Aldershot Flyer." Les recalls his childhood being centered on motorcycles and the day-to-day activities of the family motorcycle dealership: "I was brought up surrounded by the machines of the day and the smell of Castrol R wafting up into the flat above the garage, where granddad Jim and father Les would be preparing bikes for another visit to Brooklands, either for a race meeting or yet another attack on some speed record."

It was inevitable that "Young Les" would become a racer. His career started at age 17, with scrambling on a Matchless 350, but switched successfully to road racing before being punctuated by three years of mandatory military service. While serving with the British Army in 1951, Les again took up scrambling, as well as trials. He was also chosen for the British Army team for the 1950 ISDT in Italy, where he rode a BSA Gold Star.

After being demobilized in 1952, Les went back to scrambles. His return to racing, using a Featherbed-framed Manx Norton, coincided with the Norton factory's decision to branch out into the dirt with its own works machines.

1

Custom-framed Les Archer Manx Norton 500s were derivatives of a single design. All weighed around 340 pounds. *Bill Forsyth*

Ron Hankins used a modified Norton Featherbed frame as the template for the first four identical replica frames he built in late 1952. *Bill Forsyth*

four identical replica frames he built in August 1952, immediately after the first Archer Manx won its first race at Shrublands Park. Norton responded by abandoning its own race program and throwing its support into Archer's efforts. Through the "Archer's of Aldershot" motorcycle dealership, the factory supplied virtually everything that Les and teammate Eric Cheney needed to represent the Norton name all over Europe.

Archer kicked off his European racing season in 1953 with a win in France. That year, Les raced in 29 races in five countries and scored 11 wins, including outright first place at the Motocross des Nations in Skillingaryd, Sweden. The year 1954 was even busier, with the young English rider stacking up 15 wins out of 33 starts.

The succession of Manx Norton scramblers Les Archer and Ron Hankins jointly created throughout this period were evolutions of Hankins' original design, with few major changes.

Hankins' custom chassis were individually fabricated in Reynolds 531 tubing and fitted with highly tuned Manx long-stroke SOHC engines. While his frames were based on standard Norton Featherbed configurations, they all used a single upper frame tube to replace the Featherbed's wide twin tubes and offered adjustment of the steering-head angle and foot-peg location. Short, stubby cross-members added to the overall frame rigidity, and massive gusseting reinforced the steering head.

This narrower frame allowed the use of a slim, wrap-around fuel tank, while the curved twin front downtubes provided clearance for a 21-inch motocross front wheel. Teamed with Archer's riding talents, these bikes remained competitive over 15 racing seasons and often competed in 30 individual races per year.

Archer's frames were all built on the same jig and never varied from Ron's original design, with the exception of the last one, which used a slightly shorter wheelbase. The first bikes used steel fuel and oil tanks and hardware, but these were later replaced by aluminum tanks, seat bases, and air filter housings, along with weight-saving titanium axles and magnesium Manx Norton–style hubs.

The custom-framed Norton that Les raced was not a production model in any sense. It was built by Les' friend and mechanic, Ron Hankins, an Aldershot craftsman who had joined the Archer family business during the War years.

Hankins' modifed Featherbed frame, with its characteristic curved front downtubes, became the template for

Archer himself was quick to emphasize the role Ron Hankins' engine development played in his racing career in 1956 when he said, "Ron Hankins is a wizard with carburettors . . . the breathing is always spot on."

The engines Hankins molded into motocross winners were basically long-stroke, road-racing Manx Nortons, which he developed to deliver around 42 horsepower with a broad, fat powerband ideally suited to motocross. They initially combined a standard, long-stroke Manx bottom end with a Norton International cylinder head.

Dust was always a problem, even though Les' team worked closely with Vokes on air filtration. Archer recalls, "The bikes consumed vast quantities of Manx pistons and cylinders, so we changed the barrel to start with a 78.5mm bore, then 79.0mm, and finally 79.62mm. Finally, as Norton's interest waned and collapsed, we asked Mahle in Germany to produce a chrome barrel and a piston, which cured the wear problem and lasted all year."

Hankins' chassis and Archer's skills were all that were needed to make the Manx a winner against Europe's top motocross professionals. The loping muscle of the long-stroke Manx perfectly complemented Archer's fluid, road-race-influenced riding style and extreme physical fitness.

The 1956 European Championship did not start well for Archer, and a series of DNFs plagued him until well into the season before he even scored a finish. Suddenly his fortunes changed, and he scored three wins in a row—at England's Hawkstone Park, France, and Belgium, respectively. In less than a month, Archer amassed 24 points and, after battling 1955 European champion John Draper for a fourth GP, finished the 1956 season as European champion. His last win in Denmark netted maximum points and the four best results Les needed for the title.

In early 1962, Archer began a transition to later-style, short-stroke Manx Norton motors. At this stage, they were prepared by Ray Petty and used a DOHC cylinder head, a compact Mahle hard-chrome barrel, twin-plug ignition, and a compression ratio of around 11:1. With these engine changes came some minor revisions to the Hankins chassis and a change from Archer's traditional Norton Roadholder forks to Italian-manufactured Cerianis.

In 1965, at age 36, Les Archer was still highly competitive. While he and the Manx could run with the best four-strokes of the day, a new threat was emerging in the form of lighter two-stroke contenders from Greeves and CZ. It was time for a change.

In 1966, he made the decision to move on from the Nortons and sold his substantial Norton racing setup to an American rider, San Francisco–based Bryan Kenney, who then committed himself to a season of European racing with the Manx throughout 1967. The bikes Kenney bought from Les included the last DOHC short-stroke, now owned and recently restored by a regular AHRMA racer in Northern California, and the last of the original long-stroke bikes, now in Canada.

After selling the Nortons, Les bought a new Greeves 360 to race the following season and intended to limit his racing to the U.K. His plans were thwarted just one month after taking delivery of the Greeves, when he crashed on a borrowed Triumph Metisse at Tweseldown in Hampshire, breaking a collarbone and a finger. He decided to call it quits in 1967 and retired from motorcycle racing after a 21-year career. Les now lives in Spain and divides his time between sailing on the Mediterranean and working on his golf handicap.

His last Norton, the final evolution of this rare species, was described by Mick Walker in his book *The Manx Norton* as "the definitive version of the legendary Manx motocrosser." Les Archer agrees, saying, "Basically, the Manx was the culmination of years of dedicated attention to detail, and the only modifications that were necessary later were to reduce the overall weight with alloys, plastics, and titanium, plus make some parts in better alloys."

That bike is now refurbished to its former glory and endowed with a patina that enhances its legend far more than any concours restoration.

Rickman Metisse

Uncompromising Beauty

The Metisse's structural integrity and its polished nickel, chrome-moly frame set a new standard for competition dirt bikes. *Bill Forsyth*

To label any motorcycle either a rolling sculpture or an esoteric design exercise is always tempting when its sheer form and balance eclipse any sense of pragmatism. Car racers often say, "If it looks right, then it usually is right," but two British brothers, Don and Derek Rickman, took this philosophy to its ultimate expression in the early 1960s.

At a time when British motocross was still called "scrambling," the sport was dominated by heavy, production-framed British four-stroke singles and twins. While some manufacturers offered competition versions of their production bikes, none had followed the obvious design path of building a motocross bike that combined less weight and greater chassis rigidity.

British bikes of the era were heavy! A typical swingarm-framed Triumph 500 Trophy weighed around 300 pounds, Royal Enfield's 500 Scrambler touched almost 330 pounds, and the 500cc Matchless/AJS competition variants nudged 340 pounds. Although this lack of focus on weight saving could be attributed to the technology of the era, it was also the end product of a British motorcycle industry bogged down by apathy and conservatism and faced with a postwar public starved for new motorcycles.

Don and Derek Rickman were already successful former factory riders when they first delved into redefining what a motocross machine should be. By the late 1950s, they had completed the first of their innovative hybrids, combining a Triumph 500cc T100 engine with a modified

The cost difference between building a BSA B44 and a T100 Triumph Metisse is insignificant. *Bill Forsyth*

and strengthened BSA frame. Dubbed "Metisse," the French word for mongrel, this Mk 1 set the pattern for countless Triumph-BSA, or Tribsa, variants that would be built by other British riders following the Rickmans' lead.

Employing a form-follows-function philosophy, the bike used the best components available from other manufacturers, such as Norton forks and a BSA Gold Star gearbox and alloy fuel tank. While successful to the point of being revolutionary, the Mk 1 was no beauty-contest winner, and its eventual refinement as the Mk 2 in 1960 added little cosmetic allure.

Only three Mk 2s were constructed, incorporating subtle improvements such as the move to a more durable AMC gearbox and the introduction of a practical, rather than pretty, fiberglass rear mudguard and side panel bodywork. Adopting fiberglass as a racing-component medium

This show-winning, ESO-powered Metisse built in the U.K. by Julian Wigg uses a Metisse Motorcycles MRD Mk 3 chassis. *Metisse Motorcycles Limited*

was considered a bold move, and it opened the door for the Rickmans to team up with former Avon Fairings fiberglass wizard Doug Michenall. In conjunction with Michenall, they introduced a number of other fiberglass goodies that were soon snapped up by fellow racers.

However, as interest grew in the Rickman Tribsas and their associated products, support dried up from the companies that had once backed them. BSA and Triumph refused to supply them directly with frames and engines, respectively. Even smaller component suppliers became evasive, with Rickman Engineering perceived as a threat to the conservative status quo of the British motorcycle industry.

This cold-shoulder treatment might have worked with lesser individuals, but it simply inspired Don and Derek Rickman further. They chose to design and build their own complete kit motorcycle—the Mk 3 Metisse. In every sense it was a revolutionary, integrated design, marrying style and grace to race-winning simplicity through faultless workmanship and precise attention to detail.

The twin-downtube frame was devoid of the cast lugs and appendages that were standard production fare on

short, aerodynamic rear mudguard. Both side panels incorporated number plates and sealed off a waterproof, high-volume still airbox. The Mk 3 was even more versatile than its predecessors in its ability to house Triumph as well as AMC engines, sourced by necessity from donor bikes.

With its introduction, the Rickmans had rewritten the rule book of motocross design. It was suddenly possible for any rider to construct an ultracompetitive 500cc purpose-built motocross race bike that weighed under 300 pounds. Don and Derek Rickman's continuing race successes simply added endorsement to a design that did not have to be compromised to satisfy aesthetic needs.

Ironically, the Rickman brothers had little apparent desire to enter the big world of commercial motorcycle manufacturing, even with a design as unique as the Metisse. Instead, they shopped it around to the major players of the British motorcycle industry, including those very same companies that had refused to supply them with engines or frames.

Triumph, Norton, BSA, and AMC were each offered the rights to acquire complete Metisse production under its own name. No one was bold enough to take up the deal that would have given any manufacturer a quantum advantage in the marketplace. Driven by a combination of peer pressure and their own independence, the Rickmans put the Mk 3 into very limited production in April 1962, building just six chassis kits and making them available to friends and racing associates.

In little over a year, growing demand for the new model coincided with a mood swing at AMC to help accelerate Metisse production. AMC was in a tight spot and made a deal to supply Matchless G80CS and G85CS singles as well as Norton Twins, giving the Rickmans the flexibility they needed for future growth. A Metisse buyer no longer had to source a "donor" bike just for the sake of an engine.

While the Triumph-engined Metisse may have been dead from a commercial perspective, that did not deter Don Rickman from rubbing salt in Triumph's wounds by way of a final, dominating assault on the 1966 British 500 Grand Prix on his favorite T100-engined Metisse. Don and Derek

even the most refined "competition" models from the major motorcycle manufacturers. Crafted in lightweight Reynolds 531 and bronze welded to perfection, the Metisse Mk 3 frame carried its oil in the main cradle and featured accurate and fast rear-wheel adjustment by way of a cam and offset spindle, mounted at the swingarm pivot. Nickel plating was the crowning glory for a frame that was lighter and more rigid than anything previously available. It weighed just 24 pounds.

Topping off this engineering finesse was the Doug Michenall–designed fiberglass bodywork that has since become synonymous with the grace and purpose of the Metisse design. A lightweight, sculptured fuel tank flowed into a two-piece seat and tail unit that incorporated a then went on to win the new 750cc FIM Coupe d'Europe in its inaugural year, with Derek on a new 600cc-engined Matchless Metisse that had been developed the previous winter and Don favoring his 650cc unit Triumph.

Even though the Rickmans could not offer their Mk 3s with new Triumph engines, that did not slow demand for variants such as the 650cc Triumph. Would-be Triumph Metisse owners seemed willing to source their own engines. The big-bore 600 Matchless proved equally popular.

The rapid growth of Rickman Engineering kept Derek away from motocross during 1967. It was a critical time, when the mood within the marketplace was for lighter, better-handling bikes. Four-strokes were already a seriously endangered species, and the company needed to diversify with new lightweight models to survive.

Nevertheless, Derek persisted with one further and final refinement of the classic Metisse four-stroke. The Mk 4 Metisse appeared at the Earls Court Motor Show in late 1966 designed to accept not only the similarly proportioned Triumph 500 and BSA Victor 441 four-stroke engines but also two-strokes of up to 360cc.

While extending the life of its highly successful four-stroke machine, Rickman Engineering had also begun to expand its range. The business now had a 30-man work force and was producing around 25 motorcycles per week. As motocross became increasingly dominated by two-strokes, the Rickmans responded with variants, including Zundapp, Montesa, and even Yamaha- and Hodaka-engined models. By the mid-1970s, their lineup included motocross and ISDT-inspired enduro models as well as variants for police and military use. During a four-year period between 1970 and 1974, Rickman Engineering Limited manufactured no fewer than 12,000 125cc and 250cc motorcycles. Most were exported to the U.S.A.

Even though the four-stroke was long dead, Rickman Engineering survived until the 1980s, with its focus shifted away from motocross models. The Metisse was no more than a forgotten relic as young racers embraced a new generation of long-travel-suspension, two-stroke machines.

In 1983, Pat French purchased all Rickman tooling, including the Mk 2 and its chassis jigs and production rights. He revived and sustained Metisse production for 15 years under the MRD Metisse banner. Pat faithfully reproduced all the original four-stroke Metisse range, keeping the Metisse mystique alive as interest grew in the emerging sport of classic motocross. In 1999, MRD Metisse was absorbed within a new company, Metisse Motorcycles, which continues production at Faringdon, England. Pat French is no longer associated with Metisse, the classic British motocross machine that he resurrected single-handedly.

Current Metisse kit builders easily achieve a target weight of under 300 pounds. All components are readily available. *Jeremy Holland*

Cheney BSA Gold Star 500

The Master's Touch

Fred Mork's Cheney Gold Star was built with the skill of an engineer and the sensitivity of an artist. *Bill Forsyth*

When it came to selecting motorcycles, the late Steve McQueen had a virtually unlimited choice. McQueen's passion for dirt bikes was fueled not only by his own wealth but also by offers from motorcycle manufacturers seeking the film star's endorsement. During his life, McQueen was associated with Husqvarna and Honda, but British bikes remained his personal obsession. They were a direct result of his own desert racing days and his experience as a member of the 1964 U.S.A. ISDT team riding a Triumph TR6B.

What mattered to McQueen was that he had the best motorcycles available, and his favorite choice was no end product of a major manufacturer's assembly line. Only a single master craftsman, Britain's Eric Cheney, could satisfy his demands for flawless construction quality and chassis integrity. When Steve McQueen bought his own motorcycles from Eric Cheney, he happily paid full ticket price.

Eric Cheney left far more than a legacy of slim, nickel-plated motocross machinery when he died in late 2001 at age 77. His passing marked the closing of an era—one in which his unique combination of talents could find commercial expression beyond the limits of a corporate culture.

More than one writer has referred to Eric Cheney as an "artist engineer"—a title that implies an individualistic Renaissance man committed to perfection.

Eric Cheney was one of the most talented of a small group of British artisans who have woven their magic with Reynolds 531 tubing and nickel-bronze welding. The simple

Eric Cheney and the British motorcycle industry are now gone, but classic Cheney craftsmanship lives on under Eric's son, Simon. *Bill Forsyth*

21

This Cheney Gold Star built by Fred Mork weighs 289 pounds, 30 pounds lighter than a Honda XL350.
Bill Forsyth

letterhead for his business, "Inter Moto," which survives under the management of his son, Simon, does not do justice to Cheney's many achievements as a manufacturer and a naturally intuitive designer. These include a British 500cc MX Championship, second placing in both Swiss and U.S. GPs, and a coveted Manufacturers Team Award for his work on the 1971 British ISDT Team Cheney Triumphs. Eric Cheney built 12 replicas of the British team bikes. With a choice of either 490cc or 504cc Triumph engines, they weighed just 285 pounds.

Many of Cheney's creations are now as famous as their riders, such as the Cheney Gold Stars of Jerry Scott and Keith Hickman and the 235-pound JBR, or John Banks Replica, which used a 40-horsepower, Cheney-tuned BSA B50 engine. Cheney even built a chassis for Suzuki in 1968 that was used with one of Olle Petters-son's GP motors and Cheney's own magnesium hubs and lower fork legs. Look closely at Suzuki's own works RH models and it's obvious that Suzuki engineers were highly impressed by Cheney's design.

Cheney frames have frequently been labeled works of art. No one taught Eric Cheney how to design a motorcycle. His own inherent sense of aesthetics and natural genius were all he needed, along with the most basic of production resources. Cheney motorcycles were created in a space smaller than many household garages today!

Although some comparison to the Rickman Metisse is inevitable, the archetypal Cheney frame weighed around five pounds less than the Metisse equivalent but carried its engine oil in a similar manner in the upper and cradle downtubes. So fanatical was Cheney for engineering accuracy that he chose to bore his own billet forks on an Eldorado gun drill to achieve exacting tolerances.

Engineering excellence and aesthetics drove Eric Cheney far more than commercial success. His volatile personality effectively excluded him from ever taking his designs to a more commercial level and frequently tested his relationships with suppliers, distributors, and even individual customers. At one stage, after lengthy negotiations with BSA to purchase 500 motocross engines to build into his own chassis, Eric Cheney simply lost interest in the project. He walked away from the realities of production after completing just over 200 of the Heanes Thumpers that he had contracted to market through British BSA dealer Ken Heanes. The project simply ground to a halt.

If the Cheney chassis is a classic motocross icon, so too is the BSA Gold Star engine—a pre-unit design that first appeared in 1938. Its design saw no major improvements until the 500cc model went back into production, just after World War II, in 1950. Available in either 350cc or 500cc variants, the new engines used alloy cylinders and heads, with the larger motor delivering 33 horsepower at 6,500 rpm. The "Goldie" soon made its mark in every arena of motorcycle sport, including road racing, trials, and motocross. Its reputation also crossed the Atlantic, with U.S. wins in the Big Bear Run and Catalina Grand Prix as well as countless other West Coast events.

Development of the Goldie could well have halted at this point, but BSA followed through with a reengineered motor for 1954 that punched the 500's output up to 37 horsepower. Jeff Smith took the British Trials Championship that year for BSA, along with a third place in the World Motocross Championship. In Australia, Gold Stars totally dominated the 1955 Australian Scrambles Championships, filling the top three places.

In addition to the roadgoing models, the Gold Star could also be bought as a road-racing, trials, or scrambles (motocross) machine. One model was even named "Catalina," after BSA's dominance of the prestigious U.S. event held on Santa Catalina Island. Running 8.8:1 compression, the Catalina Gold Star delivered just shy of 38 horsepower at 7,000 rpm. Even more indicative of the power potential of the Gold Star were BSA's own road racers, which produced 45 horsepower, and the mind-warping muscle being wrung out of Goldies by tuners of the U.S. dirt-track subculture.

The Gold Star finally fell victim to BSA design evolution in 1963. Even before the last Goldie rolled off the production line, the first generation of BSA unit singles, in

the form of Jeff Smith's "Black Bess," had already begun to make their mark in competition.

Combining the magic of a Cheney chassis with the booming power of a Gold Star motor is a proven recipe for a visual masterpiece that can also be a winner in classic motocross today. The Cheney Gold Star owned by U.S. vintage racer Fred Mork of California weighs just 289 pounds dry—lighter than either a Honda XL350 or a Yamaha XT500. Campaigned regularly in AHRMA vintage racing, it is the end product of engineering talent and artistic expression. If form following function can also produce ageless beauty, then the late Eric Cheney embodied this great secret of life in every one of his creations.

Healthy spark from a Lucas racing magneto, along with compression release and manual spark advance, make kickstarting possible.
Bill Forsyth

CZ Twin-Port 250 and 360

Two Strokes that Turned the Tide

Practical considerations, not styling, dictated the distinctive twin-port configuration. *Ray Ryan*

When the Czech CZ factory introduced a faithful reproduction of its own works GP bike—the production model 250cc Type #968—its arrival marked the beginning of a new era of CZ technology. Its bigger brother, the 360cc Type #969, set a new standard for 500cc-class machines for the next decade. CZ's twin-port 250 and 360 were the final nails in the coffins of the four-stroke behemoths.

CZ's motocross history began in the mid-1950s, when the company produced a 250cc works bike based on a modified 175cc ISDT model. By 1959, this bike already exemplified many of the design characteristics of later pure motocross CZ models. CZ's characteristic twin-exhaust-port design helped overcome cylinder distortion by reducing overheating. The simple two-stroke motor pumped out 22 horsepower and used a twin-pipe exhaust system designed on expansion-chamber principles. Although competitive, the twin-port CZ250 proved no match for the Greeves, which English rider Dave Bickers rode to two consecutive European Championships in 1960 and 1961.

Evolution had decreed that it was time to draw up new basic rules of engagement for production motocross bikes. Lighter, purpose-built two-strokes were to be the weapons of choice. Within just two seasons, they would sweep away the once all-dominant heavyweight British four-strokes, clearing the way for a new wave of race bikes that would flow from Europe and, later, Japan.

What endears the twin-port CZ to owners today? Most say absolute simplicity and indestructibility. *Ray Ryan*

Gleaming blue #968 was hand built in the Czech Republic by Jiri Starec for a U.S. collector and racer. *Ray Ryan*

By 1962, CZ's motocross expertise had progressed to a level at which their bikes placed fourth in the 250cc GP series. Just 12 months later, CZ rider Vlastimil Valek won the opening moto of the Czech 500 GP, riding a 263cc works bike. It was to go down in history as the first-ever moto win by a two-stroke in the 500 class—an act that in itself would change CZ's own destiny and even dictate the type of Open-class bikes it would manufacture.

At this point, CZ had built only Open-class bikes based on existing 250cc designs. It was a ruse typical of the era and allowed factories to enter lightweight 250-derived hybrids as "500s." Predictably, this drew considerable flak from the four-stroke opposition and led to the banning of "big 250s" by the FIM, which introduced a 300cc minimum capacity for 500-class GP bikes.

Throughout 1964, CZ worked on a prototype 360cc twin-port motocrosser that produced around 30 horsepower and weighed just 231 pounds. It was a year that would punctuate motocross history and also set the foundation for

the career of a young Belgian rider, Joel Robert, who joined CZ and absolutely dominated the 250 GP series.

Robert won eight GPs during that season. CZ finished the year with five riders in the top ten point scorers. In 1965, Russian CZ rider Viktor Arbekov echoed Robert's 1964 title win. This gave the Czech factory two consecutive successful assaults on the high ground previously held by Husqvarna's Torsten Hallman.

Unlike the British factories, CZ was quick to translate its 250 works bikes verbatim into a production model. The Type #968, which appeared in 1964, was a faithful interpretation of CZ's GP expertise in a production motocross bike. It weighed just 214 pounds, delivered 26 horsepower, and featured sand-cast magnesium engine cases, a fiberglass fuel tank and guards, and a hand-formed aluminum airbox. Slim, aluminum-legged forks gave almost 7 inches of travel, and the magnesium hubs trimmed unsprung weight, even when laced to steel wheel rims.

In the U.S.A., the new #968 not only carried a competitive price tag of just under $900 but came with a spares kit that is nearly impossible to comprehend today. It included pistons, rings, spokes, gearing, cables, and a front mudguard as well as a chain, a complete cylinder, foot pegs, levers, wheel rims, and clutch plates, plus two pairs of brake shoes.

With maximum power developed at under 6,000 rpm from a short-stroke-configuration engine, the twin-port 250's broad powerband and flexibility were matched by a reputation for bulletproof internals. Restorers still marvel to find bearing surfaces virtually unmarked in engines that are now over 35 years old and to discover that CZ twin-port barrels can still blunt the toughest reboring tools.

Two world 250cc titles merely whetted CZ's resolve to stamp its name on the 500 class that had always been the domain of four-strokes. Although their 360 had been at the prototype stage in 1964, the design had progressed in works bikes for Paul Friedrichs and Rolf Tibblin during 1965. Friedrichs finished second in the World 500 title that year, behind BSA's Jeff Smith.

From a BSA perspective, Friedrichs' near victory must have seemed ominous. All four-strokes would soon be eclipsed by CZ's emerging 500-class dominance with the new 360s destined for production. Friedrichs and CZ went on to reign supreme over the class for the next three years. Joel Robert's fellow countryman Roger DeCoster also joined CZ for 1965, along with Dave Bickers, who finally abandoned Greeves.

A production model 360 twin-port was announced in mid-1965 and made its debut at St. Anthonis in Holland in early 1966. This first international race meeting for the season was a total CZ benefit, with Robert and Tibblin taking the first two places ahead of Smith (BSA) and the British CZ duo of Dave Bickers and Chris Horsefield.

Although visually similar to the 250 twin-port, the production model 360cc Type #969 was actually less exotic than its smaller, older brother. Gone were the 250's works-style fiberglass tank and guards, to be replaced by more production-compatible steel components. While the steel tank was marginally lighter, a fiberglass airbox, actually part of the two-piece rear mudguard, superseded the alloy item of the smaller bike. The new alloy-cylinder 360 engine also gave the bike a cleaner and more finished appearance than the agriculturally styled 250 had.

Beneath all this, the same 250-style bottom end lived on—unbreakable and now delivering 30 horsepower in a bike that weighed 234 pounds. More muscle didn't mean fewer manners, and the 360 soon scored accolades for its user-friendly power, broad powerband, and flawless transmission. However, this added performance and enhanced technology came at a price, with the 360 listing at US$1,295 by early 1967—a full $300 more than the 250 twin-port.

While its production model #969 was being embraced by riders at all levels, CZ was already experimenting with single-port designs in its own 250 and 360 works bikes. By 1966, they believed that changes were essential in the 250 class and retired the cobby twin-port in favor of a single-port 250, which delivered around 28 horsepower. Suspension travel was also increased, and the longer-wheelbase model that emerged set the basic parameters from which the later Falta-style CZs of the seventies would evolve. By 1967, the larger twin-port was being openly referred to as "the old 360," following the advent of single-port, 500-class works bikes.

Things went downhill, in a production CZ sense, after the demise of the twin-port. When the later single-exhaust-port side pipers appeared, they were true volume-production models, with market-driven modifications that would contain costs. However, many of the new changes, such as the fiberglass mudguards, actually added weight. A better, triangulated frame with extra bracing was introduced, but the new steel tank was bulky and heavy, unlike in the twin-port design. That single exhaust pipe weighed no less than the twin-pipe system, and the engine cases were in heavier aluminum and significantly beefed up.

The factory replica cloning that had spawned the twin port had been overridden by production realities. It was a sign of an emerging trend that would dictate even newer rules of engagement to be set by the Japanese companies throughout the 1970s.

1965 BSA 441 Victor GP

Redefining the Single

Jeff Smith gave BSA back-to-back World Championship titles in 1964 and 1965. *Phil England*

Hitting the scales at 300 pounds plus, BSA's Gold Star was no lightweight. Yet the alloy-engined, pre-unit, long-stroke single dominated motocross for over a decade and is still enshrined as an icon of British design. While the hefty 499cc "Goldie" warranted some criticisms, a lack of horsepower was not one. Its traditional configuration (85mm bore x 88mm stroke) limited peak rpm but delivered power that was like turning on a tap. Sheer grunt became instant and effortless acceleration. Improving suspension performance, or the theoretical advantages of reduced weight, never entered the design equation.

While most manufacturers concentrated their efforts on marginally improving engines that were inherently limited by this configuration, BSA chose a different path when faced with the challenge of winning a World Championship motocross title in the early 1960s. Even though BSA's Gold Stars were dominant in trials and proven winners in motocross, younger minds within the BSA factory had already injected fresh thinking as early as the mid-1950s. They created a 250cc C15-engined trials bike that evolved over an eight-year period. It was still competitive in 1963, when BSA factory rider Jeff Smith won the British Experts Trial from Sammy Miller. Jeff Smith believes its success lay in its light weight and what he termed "soft power."

Compared to a Gold Star, the trials C15 was around a hundred pounds lighter. Its success provoked similar lines

5

The production Victor GP launched in November 1964. *Phil England*

Vintage racer Clark Sumner of Clovis, California, wrapped his 441 Victor engine in a lightweight Dick Mann custom chassis. *Ray Ryan*

of thought being applied to BSA's scrambles and motocross machines. The task was not to be that simple, however. Smith was still clearly competitive in motocross on the heavy Gold Star and set a cat among the pigeons when he announced to Bert Perrigo, a senior BSA engineer, "I think it's time to do a complete redesign. We need to make a lighter motocross machine."

While BSA Competition Department boss Brian Martin agreed with Jeff Smith on the general principle of making a lighter motocrosser, both overlooked a critical option. Smith recalls, "In retrospect, we missed the real advantages which more suspension movement could offer. In the meantime, in order to keep the Gold Star competitive, we extracted more power. But still the machines were heavy and, at least in concept, becoming outdated."

By 1959, BSA dabbed a toe in the water with a few hastily converted street C15s, which they ran in the British 250 GP. As this was little more than a PR exercise, no one at BSA expected any great results. Specialized motocross two-stroke machines were by then flooding the class. Sweden's Rolf Tibblin won on a works Husqvarna,

but Jeff Smith on the tiny BSA C15 four-stroke took second spot. Smith says that the BSA "was the true genesis of the machine which eventually would become the 441."

BSA pulled out all stops to produce a serious racing 250 for the following year's European Championship—one that would allow Jeff Smith and BSA teammate Arthur Lampkin to go head to head against the evolving two-strokes. Smith recalls, "Reynolds Tubing was called in to help produce 531 brazed frames, thus eliminating the lugs and heavy-gauge tubing of the standard frames. Many other parts were refined and lightened, and the engines were carefully prepared. Slowly the machines were refined into excellent devices, but the Championship still eluded us. Each year BSA ended up in second place—Arthur in 1961 and I in 1960 and 1962."

By 1962, Brian Martin and his team had begun looking at developing a new works bike based on the B40 343cc street engine. A race-refined chassis already existed for the smaller C15, and they realized it would easily accommodate the more potent B40. The end result was a motorcycle that made around 25 horsepower yet weighed only 232 pounds. After BSA painted the engine black, the bike was dubbed "Black Bess" by the British motorcycle press, after the horse once ridden by legendary highway robber Dick Turpin and claimed to be the fastest in the land!

Smith took both Black Bess and his normal Gold Star to a Shrubland Park event. His practice times proved to be 5 seconds per lap faster on the new lightweight, despite his initial seat-of-the-pants impressions. He went on to take the Shrubland Grand National comfortably, confident that the new bike had enormous potential.

By 1963, BSA and Jeff Smith were committed to the concept of a lighter and more responsive motocross machine, so Jeff took Black Bess to Sweden for the Swedish Grand Prix—the last one of the season. Even though the Swedes had been invincible in the 500 class in 1962, Jeff took first place on Black Bess. The bike now weighed about 230 pounds and made 28 horsepower.

BSA also decided to run Black Bess, or any derivatives, in the World 500 Championship. Jeff Smith recalls,

Sten Lundin. Tibblin was champion, riding a four-stroke Husqvarna."

The 420 had become more reliable and lighter, and with Jeff Smith at age 30, it had to be a now-or-never effort for BSA to achieve the dream of a World Championship.

By 1964, the 420cc engine was as reliable as a rock. It used reinforced crankcases and increased capacity to produce some 32 horsepower in a motorcycle that weighed only 224 pounds. Although Jeff Smith is unsure of when the first 441 actually appeared, he won the last three GPs of 1964 and gave BSA its first World Crown.

BSA was quick to capitalize on the victory. They designated the new 441cc machine the B44 and in November 1964 showed a prototype named the Victor at the Earls Court Motorcycle Show in London. It was a production motocrosser based on Jeff Smith's championship-winning factory bikes—lighter and more user-friendly than anything the British motorcycle industry had previously produced.

In 1965, the World Championship was decided by July. Smith says, "Using a 441 engine, I had won six GPs, leaving no other contenders with a mathematical chance to overhaul me. The 441 I used was a basically standard engine, since they were very good, but the chassis and associated parts were quite special and considerably lighter than the Victor parts.

"The Victor was a good copy of the works machine, but it was productionized. This means that from the prototype to the finished item, there will be many subtle changes—a piece of steel bent at right angle in a jig instead of machined from the solid, electrical welding instead of brazing, standard frame tube instead of Reynolds 531, and so on."

That reality has done little to dilute Jeff Smith's endorsement of the production model BSA GP Victor as a landmark motocross design. He still rates the motor even higher than the 500cc B50 that followed.

"The 441 is what I have always described as a happy engine. . . . It spins easily . . . it doesn't lumber. While the larger B50 is a good engine, it is not a happy engine. . . . My preference has always been for a Gold Star or a 441."

The 441 Victor marked BSA's shift from the heavy, powerful Gold Star to a lighter, unit-construction design. *Chris Malam*

Left: **This Terry Mead–framed 1965 BSA GP Victor 441 built by Stewart Young of Melbourne, Australia, weighs 231 pounds.** *Bill Forsyth*

"During the winter, we raised the capacity to 420cc and were quietly confident that the engine was reliable, though not as strong as we would have liked. The capacity was achieved using a bored-out cast-iron liner and a hybrid piston. I won three Grand Prix in '63 and finished third in the World Championship, two points behind second place,

Husqvarna's Late-Sixties Four-Speeders

Stealing the Heart and Soul of America

The Hallman 250 was a genuine factory bike, with many features that were not seen until the mid- to late 1967 customer models. *Ray Ryan*

Four-strokes ridden by Swedes finished first and second in the European 500cc Motocross Championships from 1959 through 1963. It took British BSA rider Jeff Smith to finally break the Nordic stranglehold in the two following years. Change was not only in the air; it was also beginning to impact the record books.

The Swedish-built Husqvarna was methodically dismantling the status quo of 250cc motocross, with Torsten Hallman taking his first of four 250cc titles in 1962. Hallman repeated the performance the following year, before temporarily relinquishing the honors in 1964 and 1965 to Belgium's Joel Robert and his two-stroke CZ.

By 1966, a new breed of lightweight motocross bike had virtually swept away the old four-stroke regime. European names such as CZ, Bultaco, Montesa, Ossa, and Husqvarna were becoming as common as the familiar labels of English four-stroke twins and singles.

Highly attuned to the law of supply and demand, San Diego–based entrepreneur Edison Dye saw an opportunity to import a brand of motocross bike he believed was destined to steal the heart and soul of America: lightweight, purpose-built, two-stroke motocrossers that would make America's race grids of predominantly British bikes obsolete.

Dye boldly embarked on a program to import the starkly functional, Swedish-built Husqvarna and also to pioneer the new sport of motocross on his home soil. Along with MX would come a wave of Husky fever destined not

Restored by John LeFevr, of Vintage Husky, this 1967 Husqvarna 250 is one of around 300 originally sold in the U.S.A. *Ray Ryan*

The 1967 Husqvarna 250, chassis #670001, is the bike that brought motocross to America—the bike Torsten Hallman rode for Edison Dye. *Ray Ryan*

only to infect the U.S.A. but also to filter through to Australia and Europe far beyond the next decade.

The year 1966 marked a turning point for Husqvarna, with a shift to exporting beyond the confines of Europe. Just twelve months before Edison Dye's European motocross invasion impacted America, Husky had produced 300 of its 250cc motocross models, of which some 76 were shipped to Dye's U.S. distributorship, M.E.D. International. The balance went to distributors in Scandinavia, Great Britain, Switzerland, Germany, and Belgium. During the same period, the factory produced just 50 of its 360cc Viking motocross models.

By 1967, Husqvarna production had soared to over 1,500 motorcycles to cope with the demands of the booming U.S. market. Production in the following two years would further escalate to around 2,500 machines per year—six times the original production figure of only four years earlier.

With Torsten Hallman's 1966 World 250 Championship title win fresh in the minds of the growing ranks of motocross fans, the stage was perfectly set for Edison Dye's 1967 sales push into the U.S.A. He imported a lineup of European stars, including Torsten Hallman,

Torleif Hansen, Arne Kring, Bengt Aberg, Joel Robert, and Roger DeCoster, as well as Jeff Smith, for a series of races that made the word *motocross* part of the permanent American vernacular.

Now in his eighties, Dye recalls that his second-biggest race, held at China Camp some 30 miles north of San Francisco, drew over 45,000 paying spectators. A later race, staged on a farm at Broken Arrow, Oklahoma, crammed the 160-acre site with over 42,000 race fans. Three thousand spectator cars were parked on both sides of the highway, along with the limousine abandoned by the state governor—one of Dye's VIP guests!

Motorcycle magazines were quick to predict Husky's presence as a permanent feature of the U.S. motorcycle landscape. Positive reviews of the new 250 Husky's broad powerband and handling dominated test reports of the era. Here was a purpose-built race bike weighing just 200 pounds and factory-equipped with everything short of your personal choice of race numbers—all for just under US$1,000.

While Husqvarna itself claimed only 22 horsepower for its compact, short-stroke 250 engine, Edison Dye managed to inflate this by 50 percent as a "gross" figure that was listed in the specifications. Unlike motors derived from road bikes, the Husky 250 engine was crafted with one purpose in mind: motocross. In the dirt, a Husky could outrun bikes with far more power. Husqvarna never tried to convince buyers that their 250 motocrosser could be a trail bike or a weekend plaything. If you bought a Husky, you were about to go motocross racing. End of story.

Husqvarna's trademark simplicity and bulletproof Swedish engineering set the 1967 Husky apart from other European and British two-strokes. The almost spindly frame was radically improved from that of Husky's 1966 models, with the swingarm formed in oval-section tubing heavily gusseted around the lower shock-absorber mounts. A thin-wall chrome-moly frame wrapped tightly around the compact Husky motor, giving the '67 bikes a purposeful and characteristically aggressive style. Husky had created a minimalist race bike that would remain essentially unaltered in style for over a decade.

Husqvarna forks had also evolved. While earlier models were once available with Norton or Ceriani forks, Husqvarna had introduced silver-painted forks of its own construction in 1966. Mounted in fabricated chrome-moly-steel triple clamps, the '67 Husky forks were protected by rubber gaiters and carried a 19-inch front wheel. Their internal design remained virtually unaltered well into the mid-1970s.

High-quality Dunlop or Radelli steel rims were fitted along with Girling shocks, Dunlop tires, a Renold chain, Magura levers and controls, Bosch ignition, and a Bing 32mm side-float carburetor; all top-quality components that Husqvarna sourced through subcontracts. A so-called road-trail version also appeared later that year—the 250T Commando—as well as a 250A Swedish Army special.

European manufacturers would own the motocross marketplace until the end of the sixties, making only minimal changes from year to year. Suspensions, engine characteristics, and even gearboxes remained basically unaltered from model to model. With few design breakthroughs in the wind, Husky was not alone in making progress slowly.

Husqvarna production was destined to peak at around 5,000 bikes by the end of the decade, and the company's bubble looked as though it would never burst. History, however, is never diplomatic. By 1969, the rising storm of Japanese mass production was gathering force in readiness to strike the same dynamic U.S. market Husqvarna had strategically nurtured. Motocross was becoming more mainstream, and the new Japanese bikes introduced a fresh emphasis on styling, color, and perceived user-friendliness—even if they usually proved downright aggressive on the track.

Was it almost in tribute to the end of an era that Husky finally laid to its venerable four-speeds, on which the company had built its legend, just as the 1970s dawned?

The Hallman bike frame used a stronger rear subframe of large-diameter tubing, with extra gussets, a stronger swingarm pivot bolt, and even beefed-up exhaust pipe mounts. *Ray Ryan*

1967 Suzuki TM250

Suzuki's First Production Motocrosser

Even with sand-cast engine cases, fiberglass fenders, and integral Ossa-style rear number plates, the Suzuki still weighed a hefty 235 pounds. *Bill Forsyth*

By the mid-1960s, motocross was already showing signs of early maturity. A new wave of lighter two-stroke challengers was sweeping away the once dominant four-strokes. CZ and Husqvarna had both won World Championship titles, and Japanese motorcycle manufacturers were being drawn to the new sport.

Suzuki was one. A name already synonymous with road-racing success, Suzuki had dominated the small-capacity 50cc and 125cc classes in 1963 but had shied away from motocross until pressured by demands of its own customers, many of whom had taken to MX on modified Suzuki street bikes.

As early as 1964, Suzuki was experimenting with a twin-cylinder road-race-derived works 250 motocrosser. Suzuki's first motocross bikes were strictly "in-house" models. None ever reached mainstream production, but they softly heralded an imminent appearance on the world motocross stage.

Europe's first contact with Japan's motorcycle moguls was at the Swedish Hedemora circuit in 1965, with the visit of Suzuki rider Kasuo Kobo for the Swedish Grand Prix motocross.

Kobo, a Japanese champion road racer, was accompanied by Suzuki export manager Mansuri Nishi and former TT ace Seuchi Suzuki. They came along with two bikes—one a clearly road-derived T20 250cc twin and the other a lighter, purpose-built two-stroke single. Usually referred to

The TM250's image-building potential for Suzuki was restricted by low-volume production and specifications that fell way below those of a Husky or CZ 250. *Bill Forsyth*

When he joined Suzuki in 1968, Olle Pettersson was the first European rider to win a contract with a Japanese factory. *Olle Pettersson Collection 1968*

as the RH65, and the basis from which the later RH66 factory bike and 1967 limited-production TM250 would evolve, the new single used a right-side–shifting four-speed gearbox and weighed around 209 pounds.

In spite of its stylish blue and silver livery, the RH65 was hopelessly outclassed. It never made the race after losing engine power during practice. Its sister bike, the T20-based twin, proved an absolute handful, and Suzuki's world motocross debut raised little comment from the motorcycle press, apart from one Swedish publication that predicted, "Suzuki will come back!"

Suzuki's early motocross bikes were far from successful. Mediocre by comparison to Europe's finest, they suffered from excessive weight, poor suspension, ineffective frame construction, and lightswitch powerbands. No one at CZ or Husqvarna was losing any sleep when the occasional Suzuki turned up at a motocross event.

Undaunted, Suzuki continued its development of the RH. By 1966, the twins had gone, replaced by an all-new single-cylinder, twin-pipe, purpose-built motocrosser: the RH66. It was Suzuki's first real dirt racer and the embryo of the company's motocross lineage. However, first impressions failed to convert the hardened Euro racing fraternity, and the RH66 was soon destined to a life of obscurity, primarily as a development model.

The subsequent RH67 model was unveiled the following year and had evolved considerably since its predecessor made its debut in Sweden. Suzuki had even sent Kobo back to do battle once more with the Europeans on their home turf. Accompanied by Suzuki's newly appointed Suzuki team manager, Mr. Ishikawa, and a pair of RH67s, his efforts proved uneventful, apart from delivering massive R&D feedback to Suzuki in Hamamatsu. Yet the RH still weighed a hefty 235 pounds, despite touches such as sand-cast engine cases, fiberglass mudguards, and integral Ossa-style rear number plates. Opposition 1967 Japanese works bikes were far lighter than the RH67, with Kawasaki's rotary-disc-valver weighing 210 pounds and Yamaha's hottest offering ringing up a chubby 212 pounds.

It was a visually evolved second-generation racer, even though well short of the mark by CZ or Husky standards. The single-pipe exhaust was long gone, replaced by a dual-pipe, high-level system along road-racer lines. The long-stroke 66x73mm piston-port two-stroke featured dual exhaust ports, delivered around 30 horsepower at 6,500 rpm, and retained the four-speed transmission of the earlier models.

The RH also appeared in limited-production guise as the RH67-derived TM250—the first production Suzuki motocrosser to be offered for general sale. Available in the U.S.A. in early 1968, the TM was launched via color magazine advertisements that combined a California lifestyle theme and a provocative US$975 price tag. They boasted that this Suzuki had the lot: "Dual Stroke engine with torque all the way . . . works gusseted frame . . . Denso racing ignition . . . the Suzuki TM250 Moto-Cross with four years in the testing and made to move . . . meets all European Moto-Cross specs." A key transitional model, the TM250 combined road racing and motocross engine technology.

In TM trim, the RH engine appeared unchanged, right down to the dual unsilenced, swept-back expansion chambers, with road-race–style dimensions. The slimline frame was conventional, but its single downtube was almost 40mm in diameter, and the steering head was deeply gusseted at two points. Suzuki engineers may have known about frame flex, but their best remedies failed to cure the TM250's imperfect handling.

Although it was to prove a far cry from Suzuki's later RH68 and RH70 models, the TM250 was still clearly a single-minded motocross machine, not a modified trail bike or would-be road racer that had lost its way. The basic RH66-67 engine was an effective test laboratory for what would become Suzuki's world–championship-winning 250cc configuration in the RH70. Its crankshaft-mounted clutch and undersquare 66x73mm configuration were unique. The later RH68 used a more conventional mainshaft-mounted clutch setup, along with the standard 70x64mm bore and stroke that marked later Suzuki 250s.

These first production TM250s were virtually hand built and and came with a spares kit that included a barrel, piston and rings, countershaft sprockets, jets, and an air filter element—a precedent for later RH models. By the time the RH75 came along, Suzuki's spares kit looked more like a factory inventory and included no fewer than ten sets of piston rings! As sold, the TM's four-speed transmission shifted to the left and braked to the right, but a full-length splined selector shaft exited on both sides, and the mirror-imaged rear-brake controls were easily swapped from side to side.

While a few enthusiastic reports raved about the TM's "Ceriani-style" forks, these forks bore an unnerving resemblance to those of the Suzuki 250 X6 Hustler road bike, with their metallic blue lower legs and around 6.5 inches of travel. Suzuki's rear shocks were equally questionable, and the 52.3-inch wheelbase—1 inch shorter than on a Husqvarna 250—made for a nervous and unpredictable chassis.

Low-volume production afforded Suzuki a low-key entry into the motocross market, but it also limited the TM250's image-building capacity. Only U.S. rider Preston Petty received any mainstream exposure. Petty was also instrumental in refining the TM250 and then went on to compete with the single-pipe RH68 model before launching a new career as the man who brought plastic fenders into the world.

Suzuki's earlier efforts with its own rider, Kasuo Kobo, reaffirmed its corporate commitment to motocross. These efforts were the catalyst for Suzuki's signing of Swedish champion Olle Pettersson in late 1967.

Pettersson would prove to be not only a brilliant racer but also one of the finest development riders in the history of motocross. His influence was quickly apparent in the RH68, which he steered from an uprated RH67 configuration into a true heir apparent to the RH70 within less than six months!

Pettersson reflected at the time that Suzuki responded brilliantly in implementing changes that he recommended in the RH68. "In less than a month, I had a new RH68. . . .

We were ready to go racing," he said. One year later, Suzuki was delighted with Olle Pettersson's ongoing development work with the RH and was also ready to take on the motocross world. Sylvain Geboers and Joel Robert joined Suzuki for 1970 with the RH70—a bike little different from the one Olle had developed and raced throughout the 1969 season.

Suzuki went on to take first, second, and fifth places in the championship that year. There could have been no more fitting tribute to the work of Olle Pettersson as development specialist and motocross champion than to herald the dawn of Suzuki's Rising Sun over Europe.

Pettersson had little praise for the first of the low-pipe RH works bikes. He told Suzuki it was virtually unridable. *Olle Pettersson Collection 1968*

PART 2

The 1970s

1969 Hodaka
Super Rat 100MX

Simply Red

Foot pegs were on a substructure bolted to the chassis. Key parts were tough, simple, and cheap to replace. *Jeremy Holland*

Simple pleasures are often the most enduring, so perhaps this line of thought guided a group of motorcycle enthusiasts in Athena, Oregon, when they first conceived a basic, versatile, 100cc two-stroke dirt bike that would fill any number of roles—a single motorcycle that could be tailored for anything from casual trail riding to enduro, motocross, dirt track, or desert. Their criteria were simplicity, durability, and an affordable price tag that would endear their little bike to the maximum number of new dirt riders.

That's precisely why the chrome-and-red Hodaka Ace 100B and its competition derivative, the Super Rat 100 MX, earned a cult following that has seen so many of the sport's legendary riders confessing in unison, "Hey, I had one of those as my first bike!"

Until the Japanese Big Four turned their manufacturing taps on to full flow in 1973, novice dirt riders had little choice. Most Euro bikes were too fussy and unreliable, as well as burdened with hefty price tags and dubious parts and service support. Honda and Kawasaki had made only limited inroads into the small-bore dirt bike market, while the sub-125cc offerings from Yamaha and Suzuki left a lot to be desired.

This situation was much to the joy of the U.S. Hodaka importer, the Oregon-based Pabatco, or Pacific Basin Trading Company, which had begun importing lightweight Yamaguchi motorcycles in 1959. By 1963, Yamaguchi was bankrupt, and Pabatco teamed up with Hodaka,

Hodaka dirt bikes used common componentry and a philosophy of simplicity. Ironically, the Super Rat is one of the most expensive small dirt bikes for a concours-quality restoration today. *Jeremy Holland*

Super Rat epitomized Hodaka styling: red, chrome, and alloy, with bold, funky graphics. Never pretending to be a GP contender, the Super Rat was high-fun, low-budget racing. *Jeremy Holland*

the suppliers of Yamaguchi's original motor and transmission package, to produce a versatile, dual-purpose motorcycle that would slot neatly into the growing American recreational market.

Hodaka's 100cc tiddler racer hit the market several hundred dollars under anything else. About the best Japan had to offer at the time was a Yamaha AT1 fitted with a GYT race kit.

Hodaka's street-legal trail bike, the Ace 100B, was the starting point for the stripped-for-racing Super Rat 100MX, which appeared in 1969 for around $500, complete with racing number plates, outrageous graphics, motocross tires, and a high-level open exhaust that punched out a deafening "real race bike" crackle.

Once bitten by the highly voracious motocross bug, it was almost impossible to ignore the Hodaka Super Rat. If you were cash-impaired and low on racing expertise, here was the bike for you: a simple, one-size-fits-all racer that had followed a Volkswagen-like chain of evolution, ensuring maximum interchangeability of parts from one model to the next. Many of the major components from Hodaka's first trail bike models were compatible with the Super Rat, and the company adhered to this policy until its demise in 1978.

For around half the price of a European 125 such as a Husky, CZ, or Bultaco, the Super Rat was ready to go racing and could bounce back Sunday after Sunday with only minimal maintenance ever required. For most novices, this meant a between-race maintenance schedule needing little more than a chamois and a can of chain lube. The little bike's bulletproof nature and modest output of less than 14 horsepower were prime attractions to parents who could see both their bank accounts and their little darlings remaining intact until all this motocross madness faded away.

Beyond the U.S., the Super Rat was often underpowered in its racing class, in which the opposition had the advantage of the full 125cc capacity, but the Super Rat was always intended primarily for the U.S.A., and that is where the Rat made its indelible mark.

Within a short time, Pabatco was on a roll in the U.S., with sales of Hodaka Super Rat motocrossers and Ace 100B trail bikes bolstered by imaginative advertising campaigns and streetwise marketing. At one stage, Pabatco was the single biggest employer in Athena, Oregon. At a time when other brands were being stamped with bland alphanumeric names such as DT1 and TS250, Hodaka stuck to its guns with crazy, Bob Crumb–inspired cartoon images and individual model names that were impossible to forget.

Hodakas also featured in everything from enduros and motocross competition to the star-studded back lots of Paramount Studios, where *Mannix* TV star Mike Connors even managed to look the part on an Ace 100B.

Because the Super Rat could be easily tailored to virtually any sort of motorcycle competition, Hodaka's own 1972 tune-up and options catalogs listed reed-valve kits and a host of other goodies. Aftermarket specialists such as Webco also offered alloy heads and cylinders, exhausts, pistons, and big-bore kits for desert or motocross.

Almost everything about the Hodaka Super Rat defied convention. The bulbous chrome fuel tank was even referred to as a "chrome toaster," and the weird yet brilliantly simple separate gearshift mechanism was unlike anything else. Intimidating only if jammed with mud, the shifter was rarely the sole source of DNFs. Most Hodaka racers preferred to crash by pulling unsalvageable wheelies that defied all laws of physics and the Super Rat's dinky 50-inch wheelbase.

In designing the Super Rat, it was as though the motor-cycle-mad management of Pabatco had looked into a crystal ball to glimpse their own countless on-track disasters. From there, it was easy to build a motorcycle that was immune to even the most deadly cocktail of youth, inexperience, bravado, and testosterone. Styling finesse was not part of this recipe, and the Super Rat was best described as anything from "agricultural" to "uncluttered," depending on whether you were the buyer or the seller of the bike in question.

Pabatco boasted that such refinements as stainless-steel guards, chromed-steel rims, malleable control levers, and the ubiquitous chromed-steel fuel tank made the bike bulletproof. Magazine testers mostly used these features as punch lines in an increasing repertoire of Hodaka jokes. Yet not even the best one-liners managed to slow down sales of the Super Rat. That was the responsibility of motocross evolution, which saw the Rat hopelessly outclassed by 1973, when it was superseded by the 125cc Combat Wombat motocrosser.

Sadly, not even the Combat Wombat could sustain the sales volume Pabatco needed for Hodaka to survive in an ever-competitive market environment. The value-for-money price advantage Hodaka once held over other brands was being overridden by the rapidly improving

specs of Honda CRs, Yamaha YZs, Suzuki TMs, and Kawasaki KX125s.

The Super Rat concept was reborn as the Dirt Squirt 100 with a few refinements, a softer motor, and a $450 price tag. It weighed 185 pounds and slotted neatly between a mini bike and full-sized dirt bike in stature. It even had a neighborhood-friendly exhaust system and was wisely devoid of lights and instruments, which kids trashed on their bike's first outing. Like all previous Hodakas, the Dirt Squirt's air-cleaner graphics were innovative and pure funk.

Other models followed, but Pabatco needed to invest considerably in broadening its model range to recapture Hodaka's fading market share. By 1978, under-resourced after a disastrous fling with a 250 model, the "Thunder Dog," they called it quits. The company that had created one of the most versatile and affordable dirt bikes ever, the Super Rat 100, closed its doors.

Countless riders started their race careers on a Hodaka Super Rat. Pit scenes of stripped-down Rats were commonplace. Ray Ryan

1973 Honda Elsinore CR250M

A Star is Born

The Keihin carb proved as responsive and well mannered as any Mikuni. *Bill Forsyth*

By 1972, the advent of a new breed of Japanese motocross bike was as predictable as the much-awaited end of the war in Vietnam. In October that year, both predictions became reality. Although Yamaha had begun to build a high motocross profile for its GP program under the management of Sweden's Torsten Hallman, none other than Honda would steal its thunder with a revolutionary production motocrosser—the five-speed, two-stroke CR250M Elsinore.

Naming the bike after a small California town that played host to an annual off-road Grand Prix race was as bold as a move for Honda as creating the motorcycle itself: a design that broke free of the Honda tradition of four-strokes only. By early 1973, Elsinores were flooding into Honda dealerships around the world. Rave reviews in motorcycle magazines further boosted the Elsinore's instant high profile. At last, here was the first high-volume production motocross bike to emerge from Japan.

The CR was ahead of anything from Europe in terms of ergonomics, carburetion, durability, and electrics. It also set a standard of detailing that quickly became the norm for all Japanese manufacturers. At a time when many European race bikes still featured fiberglass or steel mudguards, prehistoric control levers, kickstarters that were little more than decorative, and standards of finish more appropriate for farm machinery, Honda offered its customers a true user-friendly racer.

Slim lines defined a fresh, "Japanese look." This restored Elsinore, owned by Kelly Owen of Walnut, California, is authentic and flawless. *Bill Forsyth*

Understated styling and a long wheelbase added to the Elsinore's tough, aggressive stance. *Bill Forsyth*

What made the CR desirable was the impact of its entirety. First impressions were enduring—from the sleek aluminum fuel tank, silver gray side covers, and compact foot pegs to the purposeful, alloy-bodied shocks with cast cooling fins. Its stark, conservative styling combined slippery, molded plastics with restrained, satin-finished aluminum and only the most understated corporate branding.

The CR250M translated all these components into a synergistic motocross machine, the likes of which had never before been available at a bargain price. It was the

bike everyone had waited for, at a time when no one was prepared to wait any longer. Selling Elsinores proved about as difficult as giving away free beer.

Honda had already paved the way for the arrival of the CR250M by luring U.S. National 250-class winner Gary Jones for the '73 race season. Managed by patriarch Don Jones, the Jones family race team functioned as a de facto Honda works operation. Already two-time National 250 Champion, Gary headed up the Honda team for 1973, along with Marty Tripes, Rich Eierstedt, and Gary Chaplin.

Gary Jones had ridden for Yamaha until Honda came courting in late 1972. He recalls, "We would secretly meet them at various test areas, and they would have prototypes for us to try, in hopes that we would be so impressed that we would sign on. The first bikes were actually four-stroke 250s . . . full-on works machines that did not resemble the XL250 in the least. They were ill-handling and really down on power. They were probably better than any other four-stroke at the time but not capable of winning a National motocross event, much less a title.

"Honda finally gave up on the four-stroke and had us test a two-stroke. This was the prototype to the Elsinore. The Japanese factory riders had been riding it in Japan, but they just didn't ride as hard as we did, so it needed a lot of help.

"Soichiro Honda, the founder of Honda Motor Company, really wanted me to ride his bike, because I had just won the National Championship. By hiring me, they had a better than even chance of winning in '73, and I would bring the number one plate with me."

Jones says that Soichiro Honda made him an offer that was too good to refuse, and the Jones team made the switch from Yamaha. The end result was Team Honda, and its mission was to give Honda its own number one plate, using the new 250cc two-stroke based on the production Elsinore model. The bikes Gary Jones raced appeared to be like production Elsinores, but they were significantly different.

Jones remembers, "The bikes changed all season long. Whenever we had a failure, Honda built a new part.

Whenever we found a part that worked better, Honda copied it immediately. They were like that about everything . . . super responsive. The bikes were actually quite exotic, with lots of magnesium and titanium. They were exceptionally light but unfortunately very fragile and prone to failure. As the season wore on, the more we relied on production parts for durability.

"All our practice bikes were production units, and they were really reliable. Before too long, our race bikes used a higher percentage of production parts than works stuff. We were even using production frames, albeit highly modified. We still used the magnesium hubs, electronic ignition, reed valve, and a few of the trick works parts, but for the most part, we were riding production bikes that my Dad and I reworked. I won the 250 National title for Honda in their first year."

Within months, the 1973 production model CR250M was a massive sales winner for Honda dealers. Single-handedly, Honda had redefined motocross with an affordable and integrated motorcycle that transformed weekend trail riders into hero racers. Even if the Elsinore's suspension was less than perfect, nothing, it seemed, would spoil the Honda fairy tale.

Yet in spite of all its love-at-first-sight beauty, the Elsinore was still glaringly conventional. With a single-downtube, chrome-moly frame, the 214-pound silver streak had no reed valves and used a conventional points-triggered ignition system and a 34mm Keihin carburetor that resembled a Mikuni clone.

The 28-horsepower engine was Honda's first competition two-stroke single. It weighed only 64 pounds, and the frame just 27 pounds, including the swingarm. In every respect, the CR250M was slim and compact, with innovations such as magnesium crankcases, lipless alloy wheel rims, and pared-down alloy triple clamps. It was a bike that felt even lighter than the numbers suggested.

On most Sundays at countless race tracks across the country, the two top contenders for 250 amateur-class honors were the CR250M and Yamaha's featherweight YZ250A. While the YZ was shorter and turned more easily, its price tag was around 50 percent up on the Honda's. YZs were also limited in supply and perceived as more fragile. Even if the CR turned slowly, thanks to its 57-inch wheelbase and a 31-degree steering-head angle, it was exceptionally stable at high speeds, with a suspension that outperformed any on an MX Yamaha or TM250 Suzuki of the time.

Evolution of the species quickly proved that the Elsinore was not without its faults. At the end of the CR's first production racing season, there were stories of gearbox weaknesses, and Honda replacement parts were never cheap!

Throughout '73, start lines had been a sea of silver tanks with green flashes, but just 12 months later, the mood had shifted. Honda CR250M owners had become jaded, and an emerging aftermarket was sprouting pipes, shocks, reed valves, and fork kits for CR250Ms, as well as for everything else on two wheels. Unmodified secondhand Elsinores were being used as playbikes.

Honda's fall from grace in the eyes of serious racers was swift and final as motocross engineering shifted up one more gear in the evolution cycle. Winning bikes had become faster and lighter, and the focus of builders had broadened to encompass suspensions, reed valves, and ignition systems.

Yamaha was also waiting in the wings with a revolutionary suspension system, based on the works monoshock bikes the company campaigned during 1973. Yamaha's reward for such innovation was the 1973 World 250 Championship, won by Hakan Andersson. Its 1974 production model YZs would effectively end any hopes Honda had of retaining a position of strength with the outmoded Elsinore. When the CR250M reappeared that year as the mildly revamped CR250M1, it was hopelessly outgunned by the monoshock YZ in every way.

History could not repeat itself. Not even for the revolutionary Honda Elsinore.

Within 12 months of its release, the CR250M was eclipsed by Yamaha's potent YZ250A and had become a "second-string" racer. *Ray Ryan*

Bultaco 360 Pursang Mk 7

Light Fantastic

By the early 1970s, the motocross technology race had speared off on a fresh tangent. Motocross bikes were already benefiting from advances ranging from reed valves, CDI ignitions, efficient carburetors, and durable plastic bodywork to suspension refinements such as gas/oil shocks and adjustable damping. Each new model raised the stakes higher and higher. All that remained by late 1973 was for a manufacturer bold enough to build a bike with true works-replica weight advantages.

Basic laws of physics dictate that a motorcycle that weighs less than its opposition will do most things far more easily. It will accelerate faster, stop quicker, demand less rider energy, and allow the suspension to react quicker and with more compliance. Looking to Japan for such enlightenment was still premature. Even though the superb Yamaha YZ360A weighed only 211 pounds, there was still a big gap between what the factories sold and what their GP teams actually raced. Suzuki's limited-production 1974 RN400L may have weighed just 198 pounds, but no TM400 ever left the scales showing less than 235 pounds, and even Kawasaki's KX450 was close to 220 pounds.

Pumped up by American rider Jim Pomeroy's win at the 1973 Spanish GP on a bike that was more production oriented than any Japanese GP mount, Bultaco elected to offer works-replica weight savings to its buyers in the 120/121 model series of 1974.

The Mk 7 was produced in 125, 250, and 360cc models and was Bultaco's lightest production motocrosser. The potent 360 needed no development to be an Open-class winner. *Jim Godo*

10

This superb Mk 7 360, restored by Jim Godo of Michigan, is faithfully authentic and unmodified. *Jim Godo*

Gary Flood on an Mk 7 360 at Mister Motocross round 2, Amaroo Park, near Sydney, Australia. He won eight Australian championships on his 360cc Mk 7 and recalls, "We could out-accelerate anything." *Ray Ryan*

Commonly known as the Mk 7, or Jim Pomeroy Replica, the M120/121 marked a turning point for Bultaco in terms of mass market appeal. Just like Pomeroy's helmet, the 250 was blue and white at a time when everyone knew that Bultacos came only in red. However, a red racer—red and yellow, in fact—was the flagship of the new range: a 352cc big-bore, dubbed the 360. It was not only a featherweight at just 204 pounds, but the Open-class Bultaco even scaled in at 5 pounds under the then FIM limit of 209 pounds for 500-class GP bikes.

Weekend racers who normally would have considered only a Japanese MXer started to give the Bultaco serious consideration, because the 360 was also competitively priced and backed up by solid parts support through established dealer networks.

On the surface, little seemed to have changed to trim almost nine pounds from the previous 325cc Mk 6 (M104). The trick lay in the chrome-moly frame, which replicated the excellent geometry of the Mk 6. Unsprung weight was radically reduced, not only with the anorexic frame and chrome-moly handlebars but with the introduction of

ultralightweight dual brake hubs, half width and mated to a spool-style rear hub spoked to lipless Akront rims.

Radically light it may have been, but the Mk 7 was still blatantly Bultaco in everything from its right-side shifting and left-side kickstart to fiberglass guards, fuel tank, side panels, and seat base. The entire rolling chassis was a great race package, and Bultaco optimized its power-to-weight benefits with subtle improvements to its largest engine.

The previous 325 made strong horsepower and was never noted for fragility, but Bultaco started almost with a clean sheet of paper for its 352cc engine of 1974. A 4mm longer stroke was teamed with a modest increase in bore size to achieve the desired capacity. Its new cases housed wider, heavier flywheels. Twin spark plugs were simultaneously triggered by a Motoplat CDI unit, and Bultaco stayed well clear of the numbers race by advertising neither horsepower nor torque. As anyone who ever raced a 360 Mk 7 soon discovered, the Bultaco was a match for anything from Japan or Europe on a fast, rough track.

Jim Pomeroy still believes the Mk 7 was an exceptional motocross weapon. When he first sampled the production Mk 7 Pursang 360, he was immediately impressed by the engine's "good long and smooth powerband . . . with a midrange and top end that were both very good." He also discovered that the big-bore was as agile as his 250, and with identical geometry, the handling was virtually the same. At the time, the Mk 7 was the lightest Open-class production bike, which clearly influenced Jim. In simple terms . . . he loved it!

Although contracted to ride the factory's 250 GP bikes, Pomeroy also had several opportunities to ride the production 360. His most memorable was not in Europe but on his home turf in the U.S.A., at Road Atlanta, Georgia, in 1974. He recalls, "It was the first of the Trans-AMA series races. and I was to ride a Bultaco factory 400cc prototype, but the bike didn't make it through U.S. Customs.

"I went to the announcing tower and asked if I could borrow a stock 360 Pursang from a spectator. I managed to get one just two hours before the first moto, and we immediately changed the tires, bars, carburetion, and grips . . . that was all. I placed third in the first moto, first in the second moto, and second in the final moto, after mid-pack starts. . .. They were all 30-minute-plus, two-lap motos, and I won overall on that stock Pursang 360. It was the first time that any American had ever led the Trans-AMA Series."

Pomeroy also adds, "If you went to any pro or amateur motocross race in 1974, there were more Bultacos on the line than any other brand."

The day-to-day manners that had kept Pursangs off the wish lists of many riders were marginally improved with the advent of the Mk 7. Kickstarting was still a challenge that required a combination of right-foot, rear pumping dexterity and bravery, particularly if the 360 decided to kick back and propel a rider's knee up into his chest. When cold it was almost house-trained, but the 360 became cantankerous when warm and antisocial if it had been left to marinate in premix while upside down at the back of a berm. The lack of primary (in-gear) kickstarting was never an issue, and it even had a 36mm Amal carb. After all, it was a Bultaco.

In stock trim, the Pursang 360 tracked, steered, and held a line better than virtually any Japanese bike in its capacity or price bracket. Unfortunately, that none-too-subtle point was quickly lost in history, because the Mk 7 was Bultaco's last conventional swingarm motocrosser, and most owners were soon tempted by do-it-yourself dirt bike–magazine LTR suspension improvements. As sold, the 360 wore spindly Telesco shocks. They were gas/oil damped and adequate for all but the top pro racers but were destined for instant redundancy as LTR conversions took hold.

Bultaco's big Mk 7 enjoyed a brief but magical summer, inundated with favorable test ride reports while the factory rode a new wave of popularity stimulated by Pomeroy's highly visible GP career. As glorious as 1974 was for the Spanish marque, Bultaco too was feeling the impact of the growing long-travel suspension revolution. No sooner had Pursang owners converted their Mk 7s to LTR than Bultaco's own long-travel Mk 8 models appeared.

Some equally tough Open-class fighting weapons also rolled into opposition camps around the same time, including the Husqvarna 360CR "Mikkola Replica," Yamaha MX400B monoshock, Montesa 360 Cappra, and Maico 400. Suzuki's RM370 was also in the wings.

The challengers were plentiful, and they virtually all matched Bultaco in terms of suspension, performance, and perceived techno leadership. Many riders for whom the Pursang had been little more than a brief flirtation were tempted by and returned to Japanese bikes.

The Mk 7s that survived are now treasured by Bultaco collectors and racers around the world. Why? Ask the question and the answer is always the same—the Mk 7 360 Pursang was the best big-bore bike Bultaco ever created. It was also the racer that Bultaco's opposition all wished they had been the first to build.

Sold as the "Jim Pomeroy Replica," the 250cc Mk 7 is one of the most collectible and easily restored classic Spanish motocrossers.
Jeremy Holland

Suzuki RH250

Single Focus

Magnesium-case RH engines demanded 100-octane fuel. *Bill Forsyth*

Weighing just 168 pounds, Joel Robert's 1972 World Championship–winning works Suzuki RH72 used very little titanium to achieve an astounding power-to-weight ratio. Suzuki's attention to detail in reducing weight from virtually each and every component extended to lavish hand finishing and minimizing the actual number of nuts and bolts throughout the bike.

The exotic RH72 specification included thin-wall chassis tubing, individually machined gears, and handmade alloy fuel tank, forks, and triple clamps. Its 36-horsepower, five-speed engine was built around magnesium castings and used a distinctive handmade, patchwork-style, thin-wall expansion chamber. With the unstoppable Robert on board, this RH took Suzuki to its third consecutive World 250 Championship title. It remains to this day one of the most significant motocross bikes of all time. To Suzuki collectors worldwide, it may always be the ultimate weapon.

Other motorcycle companies were quick to realize how Suzuki had optimized the rules of the day and applied pressure on the FIM to introduce a minimum weight limit for GP motocross machines from 1973. From a promotional point of view, this made little difference to Suzuki, and the company continued to use its GP stars and factory bikes to advertise its bread-and-butter TM motocross models. However, not even glossy color brochures featuring Robert and DeCoster could disguise the truth. While the

11

For 1975, the only changes were the suspension and minor cosmetics. *Ray Ryan*

TMs were reliable, low-cost bikes for average weekend racers, both the TM250 and TM400 were rarely race winners.

This credibility chasm between GP winners and production bikes was not unique to Suzuki. Yamaha had similar limitations with its MX range but had already sensed the mood of the market in 1973 by offering a premium-class racer slotted in above their mundane MX models. The YZ250A was an immediate hit, even with a price tag 50 percent higher than the MX250A. And Honda was still riding the crest of the wave as Elsinore fever continued unabated.

Suzuki was missing out on both the accolades and the sales returns that top-end production motocrossers could deliver. The gap between what was happening in Grand Prix motocross and what the TM range delivered was steering buyers well clear of Suzuki showrooms.

Suzuki finally acknowledged that it would take more than color brochures to win back the hearts and minds of hard-core dirt riders. Their answer lay in a limited-production, works-derived 250, the RH250L, announced in 1974 to supplement the TM models. In reality, the RH was available only through selected dealers and importers for use by their chosen pro racers. Price was rarely discussed, because the general consensus was that if you had to pay for your own bike, then you didn't really deserve an RH.

New Zealand international Ivan Miller used a local race meeting in July 1974 to shake down his new, limited-production RH250L.
VMX Library

At a time when the FIM minimum weight limit for a 250 GP bike was 196 pounds, the first model production RH250 weighed 198 pounds. The spares kit supplied with every RH weighed almost as much as the bike itself and was intended to keep the bike on the track for a full season of Pro-level motocross.

Inevitably, comparisons were drawn to both sides of the RH family tree. Pointing to the production TM was fruitless, as the RH shared virtually no common componentry with the TM250K. Furthermore, Robert's GP factory bike was hyped by the press as so specialized that it was rumored its engine would not even fit into a production RH frame.

Even without any subliminal reference to actual works bikes, the RH was a milestone in its own right for Suzuki, pioneering its production use of magnesium and titanium in a model that could actually be purchased. Probably the most pedestrian component of all was the RH frame—a chrome-moly steel, conventional single-downtube design, with an aluminum swingarm and magnesium hubs further shaving unsprung weight. In spite of its psychological advantage, the alloy swingarm proved less effective than a steel item, and Suzuki shelved it less than 12 months later.

Suzuki worked hard not only to minimize weight but also to optimize the RH's low center of gravity with its alloy fuel tank, magnesium engine cases, alloy triple clamps, and ultrathin lower fork sliders. Compared to any TM, the RH had the lean, hard look of a pro athlete, devoid of any hint of flab.

By 1972, Joel Robert was at the peak of his Suzuki career. There was no indication that his 1972 World title win would be his last. *Bob Winningham*

From its inception, the RH was the machine of myths. Most records suggest around 200 were built during 1974. Ironically, production was driven primarily by demands from Suzuki's Australian, British, and New Zealand importers rather than the booming U.S. market. Suzuki collectors rate the RH highly for more than just the folklore it generated. According to many, the bikes remain so desirable because of the levels of engineering expertise and innovation they pioneered, citing features such as the rotating-drum gear selector system, still in use today on most bikes.

The RH clutch assembly itself was weight-conscious magnesium. Originally developed in 1969, it did not reach volume production until the '75 RM models. This was typical "testing in the line of fire" for RH componentry that would eventually enhance later production models. Even the sand-cast magnesium wheel hubs found their way into early-model RMs as carryover components. No one seemed to care too much about such subtle sophistication at the time. It all went unnoticed as the YZ monoshock dominated the public motocross mind.

The RH was nonfatiguing to ride, despite suspension limitations, and introduced a fresh focus on motocross ergonomics. Suzuki's design priorities clearly favored the fast with the advent of the RH—riders who could make the most of the bike's low foot pegs and a seat-to-handlebar relationship that placed their weight easily over the front wheel. Fast guys found that the transition from seated to standing was a natural flowing movement, while the power flow was silky smooth and contributed to the bike's overall feel of being like a 125 with muscle.

So does this all add up to the ultimate 250 vintage moto-crosser? The elite group of classic racers who own and campaign RHs would certainly agree, with more than one stating that RH values are now totally subject to the laws of demand.

Close links with Suzuki's own legendary GP racers are immediately obvious. The main differences between the RH production and Robert's GP models are steel rather than alloy seat bases and the use of cast, instead of billet alloy, fork components and triple clamps. Production model exhaust pipes also have little in common with the hand-built, ultrathin patchwork quilts of 3-inch-square sheet metal that became part of the works RH legend. To this day, they remain works of art.

Suzuki's works bikes were also individually tuned, but the fact that production RHs still demand a fuel brew of 100 octane plus 20 percent methyl-benzine to deliver peak performance hints at strong family ties. Also essential is a dial gauge capable of setting the RH's seemingly archaic points/magneto ignition with absolute accuracy. Even with such refinements and specialized componentry, the production RH remains surprisingly simple to maintain and cursed with few day-to-day weaknesses. Unlike other vintage racers, an RH will take a clutchless flat shift at full throttle without so much as a sniffle.

The irony of the RH's brilliance is that it came along just as Suzuki was in a trough following Robert's three years of 250 GP domination from 1971 to 1973. Although Roger DeCoster continued to fly the victory banner in the 500 class, missing out just 1974 in a six-year string of championships, not even the low-production RH could give Suzuki the credibility it needed to continue as perceived king of the 250 class.

If the RH had appeared two years earlier, who knows how Suzuki's production TM motocrossers might have evolved? Within 12 months, the RH250L had been given an LTR suspension upgrade but few other noncosmetic changes. A steel swingarm had become standard equipment, and Suzuki issued a bulletin to its dealers with the new design spec so they could uprate the earlier L models. These refinements to the RH in the M series model merely kept Suzuki's name partially in the game. By that time, Yamaha had well and truly entrenched its monoshock YZ and MX B production models.

Suzuki itself was fully committed to the RM250 and RM370, which it hoped would give the company some much-needed motocross market share. Predictably, the RH250 and its even rarer stablemate, the RN400, became casualties of Suzuki's own production technology. Buried beneath the sheer volume of RMs that flooded the marketplace supported by glowing press reports, the RH was quickly forgotten. A few trickled into Suzuki dealer showrooms in Australia, New Zealand, and the U.K., where they quietly gathered dust. Alongside the shiny new RM250As, their price tags were trimmed back by the day. At one stage, it was even possible to buy a new RH250L around $200 cheaper than a new RM250A.

Joel Robert's World Championship–winning RH72 provided the formula for Suzuki's production RH250.
Terry Good Collection

1974 CCM

Jewel Britannia

Clews cast his own engine cases and then used them to mount the foot pegs. CCMs always had a strange, "off-center" feeling. *Jim Godo*

After only five years, BSA's 441 Victor was destined for the boneyard by 1971, to be replaced by the redesigned B50MX powered by a punched-out version of the B44 single-cylinder engine. Heavy for its power output, at around 249 pounds, the B50MX never cut the mustard as a serious motocross racer. Special factory versions delivering 38 horsepower and weighing around 242 pounds earned some glory, but for weekend racers, better machines were already in the wind from the major European and Japanese factories.

Tucked away in Bolton, Lancashire, Alan Clews had a reputation as a motocross rider with mechanical expertise. He raced both Triumph and Metisse machines before switching to a '67 BSA B44 Victor. Alan's preference ran to a works replica model, but BSA would not sell him one, so he opted to build his own BSA-based special using a stroked version of the 441cc Victor engine. By retaining the bore at 79mm and altering the stroke to 100mm, Clews' engine measured 490cc and was slotted into an ex-works BSA GP frame, fitted with fiberglass guards and Girling shocks.

In terms of style and design priorities, this bike set the scene for Clews' future production machines—lightweight, big-bore four-strokes that would become a legend under the name of Clews Competition Machines, or CCM.

By 1971, Clews was developing a passion for a better BSA-based racer when fate played into his hands. The

12

Clews' imagination was sparked by factory BSAs, but only his own skill and vision created the CCM. *Jim Godo*

Alan Clews' attention to detail, rather than hi-tech metallurgy, pared CCM weight to the absolute minimum. *Jim Godo*

BSA factory sold him a truckload of competition parts for around $1,800, after sales of its B50-powered bikes had slowed dramatically.

The first Clews production bike soon become reality with a production run of seven motorcycles under the name "Clews Stroka," but this proved insufficient to whet the appetites of potential customers. Within months, Clews had formalized his company structure, and by mid-1972, bikes emerged from the Bolton factory using Clews' own frames, as well as wheels, hubs, and brakes contracted through outside suppliers.

The underlying Clews philosophy was to build bikes to an individual customer's specifications. His engines ranged from 499cc to a bored and stroked 608cc. All were wrapped in handmade, chrome-plated frames of Reynolds 531 tubing and featured telltale "scalloped" cylinder fins that soon became a trademark. By comparison to stock B50s, with their 34 bhp at 5,500 rpm, the Clews-built bikes were punching out a reliable 38 bhp at 6,200 rpm. Some bikes weighed as little as 209 pounds, making them around 40 pounds lighter than the production BSA B50MX and on a par with BSA's own costly non-titanium- framed works bikes.

Up to the end of 1972, Alan built and sold 42 machines, predominantly 608s, with about one-third of total production heading across the Atlantic. The stage was set

for 1973 to be a boomer year, and Clews made the masterful decision to drop the "Clews Stroka" name in favor of CCM.

A firm believer in the sales potential of winning races, Clews' commitment to factory-based competition culminated in a supplier-backed challenge by CCM rider Bob Wright in the 12-round Trans-AMA series in 1973. Although less than brilliant in terms of race results against the likes of Roger DeCoster and Heikki Mikkola, the campaign was a marketing success and paved the way for CCM sales in the U.S.A. for years to come.

Having whetted his appetite with the Stateside success of this de facto factory team, Clews saw the potential of the U.S. market. As 1974 opened, he was ready to turn racetrack victories into sales. Part one of his CCM strategy was to hire former BSA factory and Cheney-BSA rider John Banks, a larger-than-life hard charger capable of making a factory 500cc BSA look like a 125.

Each CCM was virtually custom built, so restorations can become a nightmare. Few factory records were kept. *Ray Ryan*

With Banks came not only a depth of four-stroke racing expertise virtually unequalled at the time but also the intangible Banks mystique. The Big Man had a loyal following and personified the grittiness for which British racers had long been respected. While the Swedes and Euros were smooth and sophisticated, the British always played to win. Big John's ferocious riding style extracted every last drop of performance. If anything were going to break on a CCM, John Banks was the man for the job, and when that something broke, it would do so at a great rate of ground speed.

Clews knew that his bikes would need to be tougher than ever before with Banks heading the team, along with Norman Barrow and Jimmy Aird, and CCM was nothing if not responsive. A tiny company driven by one man and his personal credo of what a GP race bike should be, CCM was able to move quickly, often implementing changes on the run through feedback from its own hands-on race program. Clews set out to build tougher bikes for John Banks and also to refine his own '73 works machines to take their place as customer-production CCM models for 1974.

If you went shopping for a CCM in '74, you walked away with nothing less than a carbon copy of the factory bikes of less than 12 months earlier. Customer bikes came with the longer-travel (7.5-inch) BSA-based forks developed the previous year, along with conventionally mounted Girling shocks and improved top-end lubrication for their 498cc BSA B50-derived engines. Horsepower was a claimed 45 at 7,000 rpm, running on an 8.5:1 compression ratio. As always, there was a discrepancy in what the bikes actually weighed, with some reports claiming 209 pounds, while in the real world it was closer to 229 pounds dry.

The production model bikes were strikingly clean in their lines, with black-painted alloy fuel tanks keyed to blue plastic guards and molded yellow fiberglass airboxes set against chrome-plated frames and exhausts. As well as internal improvements, the engines had been given a fresh cosmetic lease on life, with lightweight side cases and a Hollywood-style makeover. Once more the foot pegs bolted into the cases, and most riders quickly discarded the stubby kickstarter in favor of a pet hill.

If the '74 CCM showed any gray roots to hint at its age or BSA heritage, Clews did a great job of turning them into fashionable silver streaks. At a time when the newest Honda CR250M Elsinore sold at under $1,000 with spares support available worldwide, the CCM carried a $1,500 price tag, with little or no dealer backup beyond the heart of the British Empire. Nevertheless, throughout 1974, CCM sales were rock steady at around 20 units per month, amid a national strike-induced three-day working week that slowed all British industry to a crawl.

If glamour ever won races, the black and yellow '74 CCM should have been a world champion, but the best was yet to come. Clews still had his trump card and would play it in memorable style. His solution was to produce a more expensive, faster, lighter, and even more exotic bike than the "customer" production models. It would be a virtual clone of his owns works bikes—the same alloy and chrome overstatement that John Banks, Jimmy Aird, Norman Barrow, and Vic Allan had helped evolve throughout the season.

Finding a name wasn't hard—Works GP Replica sounded just fine. The end product sounded even better, but was the world of weekend motocross ready for hand-built four-stroke factory GP bikes? The question proved to be rhetorical, and the arrival of the GP Replicas in late '74 reaffirmed Clews' ability as a man to play a hunch far more effectively than any committee of faceless marketing suits.

At the time, CCM had a production limit of 20 bikes per month, and the GP came in a choice of engine capacities: a 40-horsepower 500cc, or with 10 more ponies on tap from a bored and stroked 600. Dry weight was a claimed 220 pounds, a figure not too shy of the mark according to current-day owners and a benchmark that still eludes contemporary production four-strokes.

Glitzy sales brochures were never a CCM marketing imperative. The modest '74 handouts stayed with the tradition but still clearly captured the lines and stark simplicity of a bike that was little short of a true GP replica. White fiberglass panels and guards replaced the duck-egg blue of the production model; it had a deeper seat, a polished alloy fuel tank, and other subtle cosmetic touches, but the big news was the front forks.

Clews had finally dropped the old BSA derivatives for replicas of the magnesium slider Metal Profile forks his own team had been using. They offered 8.5 inches of travel and were mated to redesigned mag alloy hubs and Dunlop high-tensile steel rims, which were reputed to have four times the tensile strength of aluminum at around the same weight.

The GP model marked the ultimate refinement of CCM's pre–long-travel suspension technology: a race bike pared to the absolute basics and powered by an engine that a brave new world of reed valves, CDI, and plastic fuel tanks no longer recognized as viable.

While other manufacturers changed directions, Alan Clews stuck resolutely to his own course with bikes that created their own niche market and fostered immortal brand loyalty.

1974 Yamaha YZ360B Monoshock

The Revolution Begins

Lucien Tilkiens was not a Grand Prix motocross rider. Yet this single-minded, innovative Belgian engineer indirectly facilitated countless motocross victories for riders such as Hakan Andersson, Heikki Mikkola, Ake Jonsson, Jaak van Velthoven, Jim Weinert, Tim Hart, and Bob Hannah, along with Aussies Stephen Gall and Trevor Flood. All rode monoshock YZ Yamahas that used the patented single-shock and triangulated-swingarm concept that Lucien Tilkiens designed.

Advised by Torsten Hallman, Yamaha promptly scooped up Tilkien's revolutionary design for its leading 250cc rider, Hakan Andersson, for the 1973 GP season. The then-29-year-old Swede had bounced back after a serious leg injury in 1972 to finish that year with two consecutive GP wins and was destined to put Yamaha's monoshock technology on the world stage. Andersson started his '73 GP season on a conventional twin-shock YZ and rode two GPs before switching to the monoshock YZ for the Belgian 250 GP, which he won convincingly. He was soon on a roll, with an unbroken string of 11 wins out of 22 GP starts, leaving Maico's Adolf Weil trailing by 20 points as the season closed.

Hakan now lives in Uddevala, Sweden, and still clearly recalls his first encounter with the monoshock, but at that time he was totally unaware of the impact it would have on motocross design. "In Belgium in 1973, we went to a place in As, a small village in the north of the country, where

Yamaha consolidated all it had learned from Hakan Andersson's GP bikes and repackaged it with a hefty price tag in the limited-edition YZ250B and YZ360B monoshocks. *Bill Forsyth*

13

Trevor Flood won Australia's first Mister Motocross title on a visually identical YZ360B in 1974. *Bill Forsyth*

there was a very small track in the woods. It was a typical Belgian track—hard, sandy, and very bumpy. The Japanese factory people had chosen this place because the monoshock project was top secret, and they were very careful not to be seen when we were testing the monoshock prototype.

"My first impression of the bike was very strange. It felt very hard in the rear, and the saddle kicked me in the back all the time. In the beginning, there was too much compression damping and no rebound damping at all. It took us about two months of testing before the compression and rebound damping was working properly and we had found the right spring, preload, and gas pressure, so that I could do the same lap times as I had on the twin-shock bike. In my opinion, the monoshock was the most important step in MX history."

Along the way, Honda had also opened discussions with Tilkiens, but by the time Honda actually began any negotiations, the deal had already been done with Yamaha. The arrangement would shape the future design of all Yamaha dirt bikes: the birth of a monoshock system that then allowed greater horsepower, better braking, and more efficient front suspension design. Tilkien's monoshock paved the way for a new era of motocross machine in which power, suspension, and rider could work together as a total race-winning entity.

The year 1974 started well for Yamaha and would only get better. Pumped up by Hakan Andersson's World 250 title the previous year, along with Pierre Karsmakers' dynamic 1973 U.S. Open-class win, Yamaha was ready to pounce on the buoyant motocross market.

The company seized the opportunity to launch a pair of works replicas for general consumption, the YZ250B and YZ360B. Both combined the basic engine packages of the YZA series with Yamaha's newest monoshock, or "monocross," suspension. Only around 1,000 or so YZ250Bs were spoon-fed into the U.S. market, leaving less skilled riders completely out in the cold while the fast boys dived for their checkbooks.

YZ360B production numbers were even lower. Beyond the U.S.A., smaller markets such as Australia and New Zealand received little more than a drip feed. YZs that made it through the narrow funnel were campaigned diligently. Yamaha's importers and dealers wanted maximum bang for their buck, and the YZ360B was hyped as the bike that would bring home the trophies.

Yamaha made no apologies for rewriting the entire concept of contemporary motocross design. Here was a bike with seemingly no more power than its preceding model yet with more weight and with only a commercially untried and radical rear suspension system as its apparent saving grace. Although Yamaha had claimed that the B series was only 5 pounds heavier than its earlier twin-shock sibling, the truth was closer to around 17 pounds. Yet no one dubbed the YZB a "porker," and any thinking along that line was immediately blown away on the first lap!

Rider praise was unanimous, particularly as the reed-valve YZ360A motor was already a winner and remained virtually unchanged in its monoshock YZB guise. Blessed with lightning throttle response, the 351cc engine was capable of winning professional Open-class races. What's more, it was nontemperamental, easy to live with, and even very reliable.

More important for Yamaha, the monoshock system showed the way to a future in which engine power and braking performance could now be optimized. In every sense, the YZB was a revolutionary motocross machine. It heralded a year of change and innovation throughout the sport in 1975, when bikes such as the Suzuki RM370, GP Husqvarna 360CR, and AW Maico all turned riders' thinking to the "total package" concept, which survives today.

The YZB was the embryonic design from which modern suspension evolved. Bolstered by all the accolades, Yamaha never undersold the YZB. For most riders it was almost unobtainable and was cleverly positioned by Yamaha's mind merchants as its top-of-the-range, "experts-only" bike. This was no trail bike derivative, and it had no more in common with the MX360 than the same bore size and a Yamaha decal or two.

Monoshock YZs were boldly advertised as GP-derived production motocrossers and broke with tradition

The Tilkens-designed YZ monoshock placed works-style technology within the grasp of ordinary riders. *Bill Forsyth*

in not even offering a standard fold-down side stand. Each bike came complete with its own cadmium-plated tubular-steel pit stand and a warning notice that it demanded a high-octane fuel brew, with either Shell M or Castrol R castor-based oil.

Major refinements of the YZ360A motor were simply carried over, including the chrome barrel, six-petal reed valve, and CDI ignition. The YZB's intricate and voluminous exhaust pipe was a masterpiece of plumbing, but it was easy to remove—just three springs and two bolts did the job. There were also magnesium backing plates front and rear, along with the same lightweight YZ hubs used on the A models, making for the best front brake in the business—even if the rear stopper had lightswitch tendencies. Yamaha fitted excellent DID lipless alloy rims, which rated better than Akronts for durability. The rigid chrome-moly monoshock swingarm rode on caged needle rollers and comprised a rectangular top tube with a round-section lower arm.

Many other detail fittings were "productionized" versions of works components, all of which branded the bike as a thoroughbred with a genuine GP bloodline. The fiberglass side number plates appeared to be hand laminated and were secured by aircraft-style Dzus fasteners. Beneath lurked a pair of foam filter elements that came in for criticism—never for their lack of performance but as being finicky and difficult to install.

And the familiar YZ alloy fuel tank was retained, along with its triangulated velcro straps. In Europe, Canada, and Australia it was painted works style—white with red and black graphics—while in the U.S.A., Yamaha's telltale yellow and black survived to mid-1975. Image was as important as performance, and it was even possible to buy a rivet-on white plastic GP-style front mudguard extender. This soon became the hot accessory for all Yamaha racers.

"The faster you go, the better it works," was the old claim. While the workings of the monoshock remained a mystery to most riders, they accepted its performance like that of gravity: It worked fine, so why try to understand it?

This first-generation monoshock was not easily adjusted and required special tools plus a list of instructions designed to intimidate mere mortals. Yamaha made three springs available to simplify the task of living with all this space-age technology. A standard 230-pound unit was factory fitted, while 215-pound and 245-pound ratings were optional.

The stock spring proved heavy enough for most riders, and the YZ soon had a reputation for being stiff and unyielding at lower speeds. At times it would also "kick back" over jumps, unloading the rear wheel and transferring weight to the front forks, which were marginal at best and were inevitably tricked up with an aftermarket fork kit. In hindsight, fork diameter, or lack thereof, was more the problem—one that Yamaha would not resolve until the following year, when thicker, 34mm forks appeared on some 1975 production models.

The monoshock YZ250B and YZ360B were basically identical machines, apart from their different powerplants and associated plumbing, but the 360 was always Yamaha's image builder. It was never a bike for the faint of heart or any amateur racer who didn't fully employ its blinding speed or stretch its impeccable chassis credentials. If you couldn't use up all the suspension travel on your YZB, you just weren't in the game.

In the motorcycle industry of 1975, sales numbers drove everything, as they still do. Yamaha was never going to make profits by building limited-volume semi-works-style production bikes. It needed to build volume from the image of the YZs through more production-oriented models that combined traditional MX bulletproof values with the YZ monoshock chassis.

By early '75, the YZ had been choreographed to gradually fade from public view, to be replaced by the more "productionized" MX250B and MX400B monoshock models. Ads depicting Pierre Karsmakers on his factory YZ were used to launch production MXBs into the U.S. market. "Someday you'll own a Yamaha," they exulted. True as that prediction may have proved, it would take many years for any new Yamaha model to win rider loyalties as the YZB had done.

1975 Husqvarna 360CR Mikkola Replica

Northern Light

Unlike the Japanese Big Four, which grew to unprecedented strength during the boom decade of the 1970s, Husqvarna was always unique as a motorcycle manufacturer. The Swedish company produced only off-road motorcycles, the majority of which were competition machines, so Husqvarna depended on the sale of these niche-market models to ensure its cash flow.

It was imperative to Husqvarna to be seen as a manufacturer at the leading edge of motocross technology. Unable to bankroll a diverse range of motorcycles, Husky would derive obvious benefits by designing a generation of engines that would not only power its own GP bikes but could also be adapted to production use with only minor alterations.

Husqvarna took the plunge to produce a range of bikes for 1975 that were virtual clones of its 1974 GP machines. Heikki Mikkola, Arne Kring, and Brad Lackey had all ridden new-generation, six-speed, magnesium-engined 360s during the 1974 season. Mikkola made the history books that year with a 500-class World Championship title that broke Suzuki's three-year domination by Roger DeCoster.

The motor that powered Husky's '74 GP bikes was the brainchild of Husqvarna designer Urban Larsson, who had conceived a compact, ultralight powerplant capable of producing 40 horsepower at 8,000 rpm. With just 354cc capacity, it used reed-valve induction and was designed

Iain Wilson's 360CR six-speed Husky is a working racer, not a museum piece. This bike has been sympathetically developed with Ohlins shocks and some front-suspension improvements. *Jeremy Holland*

14

from the ground up for its final role in a production motocross model—the six-speed 1975 360CR, or "GP 360," as it would be commonly known.

Yamaha had publicly positioned the goalposts for 1975 with the launch of its production monoshock YZ models, and the technology-driven sales race was on. But not even Yamaha would actually match Husqvarna's claim of offering authentic replicas of its works bikes to the motocross public. Husky put the '75 360CR on sale at a premium price, around $300 more than virtually anything else available. Its US$1,895 price tag made the Yamaha YZ360B look almost like a bargain at US$1,600. Buyer response was predictably favorable. Would-be world champions dug deep to ensure that a carbon copy of Heikki's bike would be sitting in their garage, ready for next Sunday's local race.

Cosmetically as well as internally, the 360CR did not disappoint. It even had a special air cleaner announcing Husky's '74 World Championship win, along with Heikki's autograph. That same slinky alloy fuel tank used on the previous year's magnesium-engined 250CR was now finished in eye-catching purple-plum paint and made the only color on a bike that was otherwise silver, black, or white plastic.

Nothing was superfluous to the 360's single focus as a Pro-level race bike, and Husky's choice in ancillary equipment was by the industry's top suppliers: Magura controls, lipless Akront rims, and Trelleborg tires. Even though the Girling gas/oil shocks may have looked like run-of-the-mill production components, they were built to Husky's own exacting specifications and were designed to be mounted upside-down.

It didn't take long for the press to throw its legs over a few test bikes. Credible testers issued warnings to the less skilled and questioned whether a genuine GP-clone 40-horsepower racer could ever be the panacea for motocross mediocrity. Hack scribes were simply left jabbering, mesmerized by the 360's sheer muscle and blinding speed, for Husqvarna had succeeded with a concept the larger motorcycle companies could only contemplate. Their actual production bike weighed 212 pounds, just 3 pounds more than the same machines Mikkola had raced the previous year.

Apart from a few trick fasteners, some porting refinements, and one or two personalized touches, the '75 360CR was the real thing. And therein lay the problem, because the world has never been overpopulated by riders of the same caliber as Mikkola, Kring, and Lackey. The mostly average guys who bought Huskies did not have,

and were unlikely ever to acquire, the skill and commitment necessary to tame a works-style Open-class racer every Sunday. It may have been the bike they had dreamed of, but in the wrong hands, the big CR proved a high-horsepower nightmare. Because little had been given away in the 360's transition from GP to CR status, it made no concessions whatsoever to any lessening of a rider's resolve and still demanded absolute commitment.

Very fast riders who sampled the 360 loved it and started to win even more races. Its high-revving, lightswitch throttle response may have made them suck in their sphincters, but it also delivered all the hole shots they'd ever wanted. Lesser mortals just managed the same average results they'd previously achieved on other bikes that were more production compromised.

Unlike earlier big Huskies, the mag-engined 360 sacrificed bottom-end power in the name of the strongest midrange and top end in the business. Even with six gears to spread it all around, Husky still advised riders to use only the top five cogs for motocross. The chrome-moly chassis and new suspension proved equally capable, because the 360 also marked Husqvarna's entreé into the era of LTR suspension.

Seat heights were starting to soar, with the 360 perching its rider almost 35 inches off the ground, nearly 4 inches higher than a typical 1960s Husqvarna motocrosser. With its 8.6-inch-travel front forks matched with forward-inclined gas Girling rear shocks that delivered just over 7 inches of rear-wheel travel, the 360 flew like an arrow over the roughest tracks. It was also the wheelie king of 1975, thanks to its combination of a feather-light front end and explosive power.

Without a doubt, the 360CR was a genuine replica of the best GP race bike Husqvarna had ever produced. That it was way too much for anyone of less than expert status was neither a consideration at the time nor a reason to undermine the bike's collectible status today. Thankfully, for the majority of weekend racers, it also came in 250cc!

1975 CZ Falta Replica

The Year the Curtain Went Up

Magnesium hubs use pressed-in steel friction liners. Alloy-bodied, springless pneumatic shocks were unique and effective. *Ray Ryan*

The last Sunday of August 1974 was the day politics overrode sportsmanship in the World 250cc Motocross Championship. Blatant Cold War ideology dominated at the final GP round of the season at Wohlen, Switzerland, and brought Jaroslav Falta's charge on the World Championship title to a sudden halt.

At Wohlen, the Russian KTM duo of Gennady Moiseev and Pavel Rulev, along with countrymen Viktor Popenko and Rabalcenko (CZ), effectively stole the World Championship from Falta and his Czech teammates. The Russians' on-track strategy constituted a race-long assault on Falta, culminating in an incident that became known as the "Popenko T Bone." Many spectators claimed that the Russians intentionally rammed Falta, forcing him to crash in both motos. In response, the Czech fought back to win the race but was robbed of his World Championship crown following a protest by the Russian team, in which Falta was alleged to have jumped the starting gate. The FIM jury relegated him to second place in the world title chase.

Prior to that controversial final 250 GP round, 1974 had been a brilliant year for the 23-year-old Czech rider, who had started his racing career as a member of the Club Dukla Praha at age 17. After the penultimate GP round in Holland, Falta had been running second, 16 points behind the KTM-mounted Russian rider, Gennady Moiseev, and 10 points ahead of Belgian Harry Everts on a Puch.

15

This original, straight-from-the-crate CZ400 Falta is one of several classic motocrossers owned by Bob Voumard. *Ray Ryan*

Jaroslav Falta's personal 250 race bike was built by Mike Tillman of Santa Rosa, California. *Bill Forsyth*

Falta not only dominated the GP series throughout the season but had already reinforced CZ's image in the minds of American motocross fans. He took on the Supercross heroes of the U.S. and trounced them as well. During the summer break in the GP season, Falta traveled to the U.S with teammate Zdenek Velky and their coach, Hrebecek, to contest a few Inter-AMA and indoor events.

First up was the L.A. Coliseum, America's premier stadium event, where a 65,000-strong crowd watched in disbelief as Falta took his CZ to first place. He even beat DeCoster and America's top stars on big-dollar works bikes.

In 1974, CZ's works 250s had been far bolder engineering statements than the Czech factory's usual modest team bikes. They bristled with detail touches, such as titanium fasteners, scalloped cylinder heads, billet alloy rear hubs, special clutches, alloy airboxes, nonproduction plastics, magnesium triple clamps and engine cases, and reed-valve induction. CZ's own air shocks eliminated any need for conventional rear springs, and the factory forks delivered up to 9 inches of travel. Binding all that technology together was riding talent such as Falta, Zdenek Velky, and young U.S. pro Tony DiStefano. This was definitely CZ's year and was the perfect time for the company to build on its high motocross profile.

The expectations of the motocross buying public were rising radically during 1974 and 1975. Production race bikes needed to be not just saleable but on par with the very best a factory was capable of producing. Second-level play racers, such as the Yamaha MX range and Suzuki TMs, were already faded chapters of motocross history. Low-budget "trailiecrossers" had been replaced by productionized replicas of factory race bikes in the monoshock YZs and LTR twin-shock Suzuki RMs. Europe's finest were also right in there, with the '75 model GP-inspired "Mikkola" Huskies, M120 and M121 "Pomeroy" Bultacos, featherweight Ossa Phantom, "Vehkonen Replica" Montesa VR, and Adolf Weil Replica Maico AW. It was not coincidental that so many of the world's top riders had tagged their names to some of the most capable race bikes of the decade.

Race results alone were clear evidence that the Czech factory was capable of producing world-caliber GP motocross bikes, yet CZ had to face another challenge for '75. In a highly competitive environment dominated by major motorcycle companies, CZ needed to create commercially viable, highly refined production bikes that could compete in a sophisticated international marketplace. Its new bikes not only needed to be winners but also had to equal the world's best in styling, finish, after-sales support and good old-fashioned capitalist value-for-money. While CZ's marketing had always been conservative, this was not to suggest that the company lacked engineering innovation. So CZ adopted a classic "Win on Sunday, sell on Monday" strategy to secure its share of the lucrative U.S. motocross market.

Rather than follow the "straight off the factory floor" approach favored by Husky, Bultaco, and Ossa, CZ chose to interpret its works bikes in "Falta Replica" models that used the key components of its '74 team bikes. These production Replicas still satisfied CZ's core values of performance, component integrity, and indestructability. In nonengineering terms, this meant lightweight motocross bikes that could survive anything short of a direct hit by a main battle tank.

Both the Falta Replica 250 and 380 (also known as the 400) that trickled into the marketplace in early '75 exemplified CZ's careful thinking: bikes that were neither fragile nor delicate in any way yet translated the best of the factory's GP technology into genuine production bikes. Right from the start, the Falta Replicas made a clear statement. CZ was deadly serious, and if you'd been expecting porky, third-world creations, it was time to go shopping somewhere else. The '75 CZs were lighter, faster, and tougher than anything the factory had previously produced.

Engineering and art are not inherently harmonious disciplines, but CZ had obviously sidestepped any conflict when the five-speed 250 Falta Replica arrived in 1975. The style and visual balance of CZ's new bike hinted that function had fostered form—it looked precisely like the racer it really was.

From the bright red single-downtube frame and four-fin engine cylinder, slim machined fork legs, magnesium hubs, and satin-finished, lipless alloy rims to the fat, hand-made leather belt that secured the alloy fuel tank, this bike was built to boogie. Bikes for the U.S. market even had a plastic front mudguard!

Both the seat base and splash guard were fiberglass, in contrast to the steel rear guard, paper air filter, and steel airbox. Naturally, it didn't take long for the aftermarket to spring to the rescue with foam elements and a plethora of plastic.

For non-CZ riders, this was a CZ they could almost love, without making apologies for gumpy styling or third-world accessories styled by tractor companies.

What's more, CZ continued its longtime policy of selling race bikes with one of the best backup packages in the business. Even though the Falta parts kits were good, they were not as comprehensive as those of the earlier twin-pipe models. They were frequently detoured onto CZ dealers' spare-parts shelves, so many Falta buyers ended up with little more than two front sprockets, a few jets, and some tools for engine disassembly, all neatly wrapped like a Czechoslovakian Christmas bundle.

CZ buyers also scored Barum tires, CZ's own indestructible chain, and, for the first time ever, new alloy-bodied,

springless pneumatic shocks, which proved to be on par with the best from the U.S. aftermarket. However, setting them up required working with small air volumes and called for a special gauge plus the dexterity of a neurosurgeon. Once set right, they were the equivalent of the factory's own works shocks, giving 5 inches of wheel travel as well as being fully rebuildable and externally adjustable.

Suspension was virtually straight off the '74 works machines, with only fractionally less wheel travel than Jaroslav Falta had used on his GP bikes. Lighter than previous CZ forks, those fitted to the production Falta Replica featured adjustable air caps and delivered nearly 8 inches of wheel travel. And at just over 220 pounds fueled and ready to race, it was lighter than an equivalent Honda or Maico.

In the dirt, the 250 Falta Replica was equally impressive. Its broad powerband, bulletproof clutch, and well-matched gear ratios added up to far more than big horsepower claims, particularly when teamed with a flex-free chassis and powerful, progressive brakes.

Everything it did well was also mirrored by the larger four-speed 400, a bike that shared all the 250's rolling chassis components and soon earned a reputation for its massive engine torque. This more than compensated for the 400's modest on-paper potential, with around 33 horsepower and the same conservative 33mm Jikov carb that was used on the 250.

Never as fast as some of the top guns of the Open class, noticeably the 400 Yamaha, 360 Bultaco, or 400 Maico, the 400 Falta Replica could still be a winner in the right hands. Tony DiStefano, a young privateer racer from Pennsylvania, proved that point on his factory prototype when he fought a season-long battle against Jimmy Weinert, Gary Semics, and Mike Hartwig for the 1974 500cc U.S. National Championship. Tony "D" finished in second place that year, his performance earning him a factory ride with Suzuki for 1975. He went on to win three National 250 titles from 1975 to 1977 but still had fond memories of his CZ 400, recalling, "I could just pop the CZ 400 into one gear and roll around the track."

Falta's personal 250 features porting and reed-valve installation by Mark Alcorn, along with a Mikuni carb.
Bill Forsyth

1976 Puch MC250 Everts Replica

Carbon Copy

The twin-carb setup delivered two powerbands, to overlap and complement each other. *Bill Forsyth*

Twenty-three-year-old Belgian Harry Everts left Sweden's Hakan Andersson and Germany's Willy Bauer eating dust and scrapping for second and third, respectively, when he stole his first World 250 motocross title from under the noses of Yamaha and Suzuki in 1975. His World Championship title was also a first for Puch.

It was Everts' second year with the Austrian Puch factory, after scoring a third place the previous year. What made his 1975 victory so remarkable was that he achieved it on a motorcycle built by a company that did not even manufacture a production 250cc motocross machine. Everts' GP bike was fresh off the Puch drawing boards: a revolutionary twin-carb, dual-induction, single-cylinder two-stroke.

Even before the 1975 racing season had concluded, Everts had been in an unassailable position with the new MC250. Following the Swiss GP, the final round for that season, Puch management decided to produce a limited-production motocrosser identical to the bikes Everts had campaigned. The bikes would be available for sale in 1976, as an image-building rather than a profit-generating exercise. However, only 100 of the 250cc machines and an unspecified number of larger-engined but otherwise identical 380s were scheduled for production.

Throughout '75, Everts' factory 250, with its unique piston port plus rotary-valve, dual-induction, twin-carburetor motor attracted little in-depth coverage by the international

This original Puch MC250 Everts Replica owned by Californian Lee Fabry is one of only 95 MC250s produced. *Bill Forsyth*

16

Harry Everts believed that 46 horsepower was easy to obtain with mild tuning. *Bill Forsyth*

motorcycling press. What was made clear in the brief reports of the time was its performance potential, with two powerbands to overlap and complement each other. The rotary-disc-valve induction provided low-end torque with a smooth transition to the main piston porting, which then produced peak horsepower.

Harry Everts still has his 1975 World Championship Puch sitting at his home in Belgium. "I never knew how many horsepower we had on the bike," he reflects, "and I wasn't interested in knowing."

As a manufacturer and GP motocross participant, Puch was unique. Because the factory produced no 250cc model in any form, all design and development of the MC250 was strictly at a works level rather than geared for mass production. Any components built for the MC were high-cost, low-volume items, and Puch's minuscule production target of only 100 bikes precluded any form of assembly line. Instead, Puch chose to build its production MC250s in the same way it produced its GP bikes. Each was built individually by a team of workshop mechanics, who completed one bike and then commenced assembly of the next.

Virtually every major component was hand assembled, individually fitted, and fine-adjusted by the same teams of Puch mechanics who had created Everts' championship-winning bikes. While claims of "factory replicas" were not new by 1976, only a few manufacturers had ever come close to delivering such a promise, but Puch went the full distance with the MC250. The production bike was a precise carbon copy of the Everts works bikes. No changes whatsoever were made to facilitate production or reduce costs.

The pure and untainted GP bloodline of the MC250 was evident when the bike arrived in 1976, with a price tag equivalent to around $3,000 in Europe and only fractionally higher in the U.S.A. Only 95 MC250s were ever produced, even though Puch initially aspired to build 100. Production numbers of the larger 380cc model remain unknown.

While no one disputed the 380's reputation as an awesome weapon in the 500 class, it was the revolutionary twin-carb 250 that attracted the most attention. The individually assembled and component-matched engines used magnesium cases that were sand cast and hand finished and fitted with cast aluminum heads and barrels. It used two identical 32mm Bing carbs and combined reliability and user- friendliness with features such as primary kickstarting, Motoplat CDI ignition, a Mahle piston, and left-side shifting.

As a package, the MC was, in hindsight, the bargain racer of the decade—a professional race bike for professional racers. Its muscular, dual-induction motor delivered an abrupt burst of power when engine revs hit the transition point from low-speed rotary valve to high-speed piston-port induction. While it was smooth and rideable, with exceptional midrange-to-top-end performance, the MC250 was not a bike to be ridden in anything less than full attack mode. It rewarded only the most skilled riders who could push it to its performance limits.

Puch also understood that raw power alone doesn't mean winning. At a time when suspension development was escalating as never before, Puch chose a conservative setup that combined Marzocchi forks and cantilever twin shocks with a simple, yet innovative, chrome-moly steel frame. Its primary strength lay in a hefty, rectangular-section backbone tube that was both lightened and reinforced by stamping recessed holes between the side flanges. If this weren't enough, Puch then chose to bolt, rather than weld, the twin downtubes of the lower loops to their attachment points behind the steering head. A simple, round-section swingarm rode on needle bearings, and the LTR suspension setup delivered 9 inches of travel from the stock-issue Marzocchi reservoir shocks.

Early production bikes used 8.6-inch-travel, leading-axle, 38mm diameter Marzocchi forks with aluminum lower legs. Later bikes carried 9-inch-travel ZTI Marzocchis with magnesium legs and flat aluminum triple clamps.

"The brakes were not so good," according to Harry Everts. If the MC250 had a major weakness, it was its lack of stopping power. Although the cable-operated rear brake gave good feel, it lacked the stopping power

Harry Everts recalls, "I never knew how many horsepower we had on the bike, and I wasn't interested in knowing." *Chris Malam*

the Puch's performance demanded. Nevertheless, with magnesium hubs, Akront lipless alloy rims, and Metzeler tires all as standard equipment, the whole package was GP inspired, with low unsprung weight to optimize suspension performance.

Servicing the MC250 was simple and fast. The single Twin Air foam filter was high-mounted in an airbox enclosed by velcro-fastened vinyl flaps, and the seat was easily removable, with just one nut at the rear to allow access to the airbox. Both side number plates were integral extensions of the airbox side covers. Little, if anything, was superfluous to the MC's single role in life: to win motocross races.

Detail engineering and ancillary equipment also reflected the company's GP involvement: functionally styled fiberglass fuel tanks, holding just over two U.S. gallons of premix, handlebars in either chrome-moly or aluminum, levers and twistgrips by Magura, and translucent white plastic guards by Falk in Germany that were wide, well balanced, and reasonably durable.

Standard horsepower was at least 42, but Harry Everts said at the time that he believed 46 horsepower

was easy to obtain with only very mild tuning. The prodigious power was further substantiated when Puch's 1976 specifications listed a none-too-modest 43.5 bhp at 8,200 rpm. Other literature went so far as to list 46 rear-wheel horsepower and around 51 at the crankshaft. Such variations only added to the legend and charisma of the MC as one of the rarest and most potent production motocrossers ever.

In a production sense, the MC250 marked the peak of Puch's presence as an independent manufacturer drawing primarily on its own resources and technology. Even while the MC250 was current, Puch was also playing around with a hybrid that used the Rotax (CanAm) 250 rotary valve in one of its own frames.

The MC250 also hinted at the future, and by the late 1970s, Puch had contracted to use four-stroke and two-stroke Rotax engines in its own production bikes. Puch finally merged with Piaggio in Italy in 1991, a little less than 100 years after Johann Puch's company, which started as a bicycle manufacturer at Graz, first opened its doors.

1977–79 Yamaha HL500

Viking Raider

Front fork selection varied from bike to bike. Stock YZ components were often installed, as well as Marzocchi and works OW-style billet items. *Bill Forsyth*

In 1975, only a small handful of racers took four-strokes seriously. Fortunately, two of them were Swedish motocross legends Bengt Aberg and Torsten Hallman.

The bike forged through their collective initiative and the engineering genius of fellow countryman Sten Lundin set the parameters for a revolutionary school of thought in four-stroke dirt bike design. If today's lightweight four-stroke motocrosser has such a thing as a lineal ancestor, it must be the Yamaha HL500, which first saw the light of day over 25 years ago.

Through the combined clout of marketing dollars and sheer bravado, Yamaha had pushed four-strokes back into fashion by the mid-1970s. With the launch of the XT500 trail model in late 1975, the company unknowingly set the stage for a GP motocross assault that would culminate in one of the most revolutionary limited-production Yamaha race bikes of all time.

By no stretch of the imagination would Yamaha's bulky 305-pound XT500 be anything more than a mild-mannered road/trail bike. Powered by an understressed, two-valve, 499cc single-cylinder engine with design roots back to the XS650 road bike, the XT was the most unlikely basis for an exotic GP motocross bike.

Yamaha soon delved into the concept of a stripped-down XT, but its end product fell way short of the mark for serious racing. Shortly after the XT's release, Yamaha dipped into its MX model parts bins in 1976 for forks and

17

A Husqvarna-derived chassis and Yamaha's tough TT/XT500 OHC motor made for a potentially competitive package. The HL500 ridden by Bengt Aberg soon served notice to the all-conquering two-strokes. *Bill Forsyth*

The HL500's weight could be trimmed to around 245 pounds—right in line with current-era four-stroke YZs. *Bill Forsyth*

Right: The ProFab-framed HL500 raced by Ricky Johnson from 1981 to 1984 weighed just 246 pounds, with a whopping 51.5 horsepower. *Ray Ryan*

suspension to create a "playbike" variant, the TT500C. Even though it weighed around 33 pounds less, that was still nearly 270 pounds.

At a time when Yamaha's own YZ400C weighed 230 pounds, even the most creative copywriters couldn't disguise the fact that the TT was never to be a racer. However, the combined impact of both bikes was to spark an aftermarket industry that soon offered everything for TT500s from aluminum swingarms, Mikuni kits, cams, pipes, and external oil feeds to Marzocchi forks.

Even the most radically modified, standard-framed TT500s were never competitive in motocross. The excess weight and poor chassis geometry that were the prime limitations did not go unnoticed by Swedish engineer Sten Lundin, a former 500cc motocross world champion (1959 and 1961). Lundin saw the potential of the four-stroke Yamaha 500 engine and purchased an ex-ISDT XT500 prototype from an American privateer in late 1975. He immediately started his own motocross project, fitting the Yamaha engine to a Husqvarna motocross frame.

In January 1977, Bengt Aberg tested the new bike for the first time and loved it immediately. This bike was sent to the U.S.A., where specialty shop ProFab built a new lightweight chassis while Aberg was in the U.S. testing different carbs, cams, and suspension.

Yamaha was keen to launch its XT500 production model in Europe and realized that kudos gained in international motocross carried a lot of muscle on the sales floor. The company saw a window of opportunity in early 1977, when Lundin and Hallman approached Yamaha for backing to fund a serious GP challenge with the hybrid thumper.

The decision was made for Aberg to ride the bike in the 500 cc GP class with support from Swedish Yamaha importer Hallman and Eneqvist, one of Torsten Hallman's business enterprises, and some help from Yamaha Europe N.V. While the Swedes could see great potential for a competitive four-stroke bike, Hallman had sold Yamaha management on the PR impact of targetting the HL for at least one GP win in the coming season.

In the transition from its original Husqvarna roots, the design quickly evolved through ProFab, emerging with a new, lightweight frame that would become the basis of a limited-production Yamaha model. In conjunction with business associate Torsten Hallman, Lundin had already used ProFab to supply frames, stands, and other items for their own Husqvarna bikes. They had every confidence in the California-based speciality shop, with its reputation for quality, lightweight race components.

The new Hallman-Lundin Yamaha 500 project quickly evolved to a specification that included an aluminum swing-arm and state-of-the-art Fox Air Shox. They dubbed it the HL500, combining the initials of both their family names.

By late 1977, the original design had further evolved with the use of lightweight production-model YZ hubs and forks plus dual engine mounting plates and hardware. At just 225 pounds, it was a full 45 pounds lighter than the standard TT500, with around 10 inches of wheel travel front and rear.

Lundin then turned Swedish tuning ace Nils Hedlund loose on the motor, who gave it an 11:1 compression ratio, a larger 36mm Mikuni carb, and changes to ignition and clutch assemblies. Hedlund left the bottom end of the tough XT/TT powerplant completely untouched.

The HL500 soon earned the nickname of "Aberg Yamaha" in the motorcycle media. Aberg finally capped off an otherwise lackluster season with a GP win in Luxembourg late that year, but Yamaha elected to drop the project and would not support a future four-stroke team, even though Bengt Aberg experimented with a three-valve cylinder head designed by Nisse Hedlund, in his HL500 during 1978.

Nevertheless, the machine had attracted the attention of Yamaha's own European motocross team boss, who

opted to create a small production run of HL500 replicas. The Norton factory at Shenstone (U.K.) was asked to build the bikes, using a cosmetically modified TT500 engine and a chassis based on the one used by Aberg the previous year.

Although they lacked serious GP-winning performance, 200 HLs rolled out the Norton factory doors in the first year of production. The process was repeated in 1979 with a further run, featuring wilder camshafts, improved CDI ignitions, and 38mm Mikuni carbs. Minor changes to the swingarm shock mounts upped rear-wheel travel to 10 inches, while adopting Yamaha YZ400F forks delivered around 10.5 inches up front.

European production totaling 400 bikes over two years was inevitably topped up in other markets with a surge in aftermarket-framed specials. Many claimed either inspiration or heritage from the HL500. In the real world of racing, these bikes were often on a par with or even better than the HL "production" machines, but few survive to be prized as highly as the two Norton-built models.

Bengt Aberg finished the 1977 season in ninth spot in the 500 GP class but slipped back to thirteenth the following year. *Nisse Wedin Collection 1978*

Brad Lackey's Honda RC450-78

Horsepower Heaven

In 1979, Britain's Graham Noyce gave Honda its first of three consecutive 500 World Championship wins with the mighty RC450-79. However, the RC450-78 that preceded Honda's 1979 world beater remains the bike more often remembered around bars and barbecues.

A classic example of horsepower overkill, the imperfect yet beautiful RC-78 earned Honda second spot on the World 500 Championship points table in 1978. The man who put it there that year was then 25-year-old American star Brad Lackey, who had recently moved from Husqvarna following earlier team stints with CZ and Kawasaki.

When Honda came knocking on Brad's door in 1977, he was looking for a World Championship–winning season. Although nothing less would suffice for the young Californian, Lackey did not take the number one spot that year but topped his first Honda season with a well-deserved fourth aboard the RC400-77. It was a hint of greater things to come.

Honda committed itself totally to the 1978 World Championship, with Brad Lackey joined by hard-charging, fast-living Englishman Graham Noyce—21 years of age. The duo was a dynamic and promotable commodity. Noyce's talent was never questioned, while Lackey's reputation was enhanced by his Farleigh Castle (U.K.) performance the previous year and his subsequent status as the first American to ever win a 500 GP. As the 1978 season opened, Honda's team was as good as any and better than most.

The only production Honda CR parts used on the RCs were the seat and mudguards. Everything else was either cast, machined, milled, fabricated, or otherwise formed by hand. *Bill Forsyth*

RC450s reputedly cost Honda around US$80,000 each. *Bill Forsyth*

89

This ex-Lackey RC is unrestored and embodies Honda's take-no-prisoners GP philosophy. *Bill Forsyth*

Earlier rumors abounded that Honda would have the hot machinery for '78—lighter, more powerful, and with even more suspension travel than the 12 inches of the RC400-77 that had paved Honda's way into 500GP motocross.

What was expected was not what Honda delivered when the RC450-78 was unveiled. Hand built, exotic, and horrendously expensive to produce, at a rumored US$80,000 apiece, the 209-pound RC-78 at first seemed almost a retrograde design. Despite many hi-tech titanium components, the 78 had shorter suspension travel and a nonfloating rear brake, and its weight saving was far from remarkable. Where it did not compromise was in horsepower, with around 63 horses claimed for the 450cc five-speed engine.

"In order to ride this bike aggressively, you needed to be the strongest or baddest rider on the track," according to Brad Lackey, who still rates the RC450-78 as "a bike which was as good as anything on the track at the time." He recalls, "Honda's European headquarters were in Offenbach, Germany, and I was testing the new RC450-78 at most of the local tracks and off on the weekends to the biggest international meets. I recall that the horsepower was the best usable power with tons of torque . . . more than any previous motor that I tested. The bike frame was very rigid. There was no flex at all, and the suspension was as good as anything at that time."

In the off-season, Lackey had traveled to Japan for R&D work with Honda on the RC450. He says, "The motors were perfect right from the start. This is by far the bike that needed the least amount of R&D that I have ever raced. I knew from the first ride that it would be competitive with its power and powerband. We never checked the power data, but 60 to 65 horsepower seems right."

Honda's longtime obsession with Formula 1–style racing technology adopted to motocross was clearly evident throughout the eight RC-78s the factory built. At the time, the RC-78 marked the pinnacle of Honda's design and manufacturing capacity, with features such as sand-cast magnesium engine cases and a black magnesium-alloy carburetor. All gearbox components were handmade, as were the crankshaft and most internal engine components. Honda claimed that the only production CR parts used on the RCs were the seat and mudguards. Everything else was either cast, machined, milled, fabricated, or otherwise formed by hand—right down to billet alloy axle adjusters and control cables with stainless-steel internals.

Sand-cast magnesium hubs were used on both wheels, along with hand-crafted, dual-tract fiberglass air-boxes and an abundance of titanium fasteners, at a time when such exotica were not even commonplace in F1. Up front, Honda used 41mm-diameter forks—considered huge when the bike first appeared—teamed with rear Fox Air Shox by Moto-X Fox. This setup soon became Honda's de facto works standard. Lackey recalls that few major changes were made to the bike during the 1978 season and that only the Fox shocks, or any parts that broke, were redesigned. Other parts were merely changed regularly.

Lackey threw down the challenge early in 1978, taking the new RC to wins in Austria and France as well as repeating his previous season's outright domination of the British 500 GP at Farleigh Castle. With his fellow former Husky rider, Finland's Heikki Mikkola, pushing hard to extend his lead throughout the season in the hope of giving Yamaha two consecutive 500 World Championship titles, Lackey had to settle for second places in Denmark, Finland, Sweden, Italy, and Belgium.

A series of mechanical problems and crashes compounded his efforts, and any remaining luck came to an abrupt end in August, when he crashed at the start of the last GP of the season in Luxembourg, losing any chance of winning the World Championship. Lackey flew home injured and missed the Motocross des Nations at Gaildorf in Germany in September.

U.S.A. Honda team rider Tommy Croft flew over to Europe and took over Lackey's RC. The Americans seemed poised for victory as they tied with the Russian team at the end of the first moto. However, just 10 minutes later, Croft's RC blew a front tire, and all American hopes of a first MXdN win evaporated instantly. The day also marked the end of the RC-78's race career. By October, Lackey had shifted back to Kawasaki and was already planning his '79 season with a new UniTrak works 440.

His RC-78 vanished from the international motocross scene and has never been ridden since Tommy Croft's fateful day. After the MX des Nations in '78, two RC450s were packed in Lufthansa air freight crates for their return to the U.S.A. and labeled "Return to American Honda," with the intention that Lackey would ride them later in the Trans-AMA series. They had been serviced and were even fitted with new tires.

After their arrival in the U.S., both bikes eventually found their way into a desert warehouse owned by the late Al Baker. Following Baker's death in a helicopter accident in 1991, they languished there for some time before an American collector negotiated with the Baker family for their sale. The new owner found them exactly as they had been shipped from Europe, complete with air freight labels and ready to race.

In more recent times, the Lackey bike was sold to another collector and remains unrestored, with only the addition of a set of rear number plates to enhance the RC's character and raw beauty. Even the grips are as they were.

Today, Lackey still rates the RC450-78 as one of the true milestones in motocross design. "Of course, Joel's Suzukis are number one, but the Hondas would be number two, especially in the 500 class. . . . The RC450-78 was the best bike that year . . . even if it was a bit too tall!"

Factory engine numbers leave no doubt as to the integrity of the surviving RC450-78s. *Bill Forsyth*

1978-80 Honda CR250R

Red Revolution

Showa suspension components were the CR's biggest weakness. Aftermarket rear shocks were at the top of most riders' shopping lists. *Bill Forsyth*

It is ironic that the very motorcycle that launched Honda into the motocross market was almost to prove the company's undoing just a few years later. Honda's massive investment in the first model CR250M Elsinore came back to haunt the company in the four years from 1973. With development funds tied up, and unwilling to make production changes, Honda reluctantly marked time while opposition motorcycle manufacturers leapt forward with new motocross suspension and engine technology.

Yamaha assumed the high ground in motocross sales with the introduction of the monoshock YZ250B and YZ360B in 1974 and was followed by Suzuki's launch of the RM250A and RM370A in late 1975. By comparison, Honda had no Open-class production bike, and its subsequent models of the original Elsinore CR250M had become as popular as warm beer. Only the aftermarket really kept CR250s on the track, thanks to a variety of tuning kits and chassis modifications.

By contrast, Honda's commitment to GP and Supercross went from strength to strength, but its lineup of factory motocrossers bore little resemblance to the production CRs cluttering Honda dealerships. Honda was to invest four seasons in its revolutionary factory race bikes, even though it did not have a competitive production 250 to offer buyers. What Honda raced was not what it offered for sale to weekend motocross racers.

The benefits of factory involvement with riders such as Marty Smith, Billy Grossi, Rich Eierstedt, Tommy

The 1978 model "Red Devil" CR250R (rear) was Honda's first major design change since the original CR250M and was closely based on the Type 11 RC250-77 factory bikes. *Bill Forsyth*

Porting changes on the 1980 model transformed the CR250R from a high-rpm screamer into a short-shifting torque machine. *Bill Forsyth*

Croft, and Jim Pomeroy would not be realized until late 1977 with the U.S. introduction of the new CR250R. The new CR125RZ was still almost two years off.

Visually, the bikes were little short of stunning. Their all-red paint scheme boldly proclaimed their works bike heritage and immediately branded the R series as a turning-point model for Honda. On sale in early 1978 in most markets, the "Red Devil" CR250Rs were closely based on the Type 11 RC250-77 factory bikes. This connection was far more than just cosmetic. Honda's own riders often used production CR250Rs instead of the more exotic and expensive RCs in Supercross and U.S.A. 250-class National races. The most obvious difference was the suspension—Showa on the production CR250R and usually Moto-X Fox on the works bikes.

In early 1978, Marty Tripes proved the hardcore competitiveness of the CR250R when he came back to Honda and took out the Daytona Supercross on a production bike. Throughout that year, Tripes was consistently quick whenever he rode the production CR and frequently raced head to head against Yamaha's Bob Hannah on a monoshock OW38 that was reputed to weigh just 198 pounds.

From Day 1, the red racers earned a reputation for horsepower. This was acclaimed unanimously by dirt-bike testers from the major magazines and reinforced by Honda's return to the winner's podium at weekend race tracks. It was not uncommon to see the Honda crowned as the horsepower king in a multibrand 250 shootout, thanks to its 36-horsepower, reed-valve engine. The chromed cylinder liners were seemingly bulletproof by comparison to earlier offerings from other factories, while Honda's old CR250 gearbox bogeyman had finally been buried once and for all. Reliability played a major role in the CR's appeal.

So had Honda finally realized that mainstream competitors rarely pampered its production motocross bikes? The red CR250Rs rarely broke and were capable of surviving that almost total lack of between-race maintenance only young racers could inflict. At best, an essential heavy-maintenance program comprised cleaning the air filter, lubing the #528 drive chain, and buffing the paintwork. Wheel and hub assemblies were racer tough, and Honda sold few replacements.

The Showa front forks were a slightly different story. They suffered Honda CR traditional harshness, and the front springs sagged out early in their life. Offering 12 to 13 inches of travel, the forks may have been durable, but they allowed no adjustment to ride height or spring rate.

Years spent inadvertently bankrolling the aftermarket had left many Honda owners with an insatiable passion to refine and modify their bikes. The CR250R did not make them break with tradition. Most CR250R riders agreed that all they really needed was a little help for the Showa forks and some improved rear shocks. Fixing the front end could be done with a phone call to any one of a number of suppliers of spring kits, revalves, and air caps.

Moto-X Fox suspension was the choice of the day, particularly with the advent of Fox's own complete front fork assemblies in 1979 and the distinctively machined, alloy-bodied Fox Air Shox, which sold for around US$300. Fox Air Shox used no separate springs and offered the optimum rear-end package when combined with a lightweight aluminum swingarm. This usually added up to 2 inches to the wheelbase and gave the rider a choice of 12- or 13-inch shocks. While Fox's long-travel aftermarket forks will seem cheap by today's standards at under US$500, few amateur riders could justify the expense at a time when standard CR forks could be upgraded for around $100.

Other modifications were readily available, particularly with consumer-level R&D trickling down through magazine features of Honda's ever-evolving factory bikes. Upper chain rollers and heavy-duty, aluminum-plate lower chain guides and upper engine braces could be bought as kits, along with aluminum rings that reinforced the air filter mount. However, the reality was that the production CR250R did not require much real help to stay together.

Even heavy-duty clutch plates were sought out only by serious gunfighters. Full floating-rear-brake conversions, based on the factory RC setups, were considered almost overkill, and from a contemporary perspective, the equipment normally available was minimal for what was then a state-of-the-art contemporary race machine.

Nothing was broken, so little needed to be fixed when Honda freshened up the original CR250R package in the 1979 model. Subtle changes to porting and the reed valves boosted the maximum horsepower fractionally to a claimed 37 bhp at 7,500 rpm and smoothed delivery with stronger bottom-end and midrange muscle. Few tuners suggested modifications to an engine that had proven to be a great race weapon, while even Honda's own team riders candidly admitted that their own CR250R motors were virtually dead stock.

With its single downtube frame, the CR250R was to remain basically unchanged from its launch through to 1980, when a twin-downtube cradle frame was introduced, along with significant motor changes. Nevertheless, it was time for Honda to empty out both the baby and the bathwater. Or was it just a case of changing one component too many and ending up with a brand-new bike?

This was effectively the story with the CR250R 80. Honda responded to frame geometry criticism by moving

Honda's CR250R formula was simple: solid race bikes that could win Sunday races for weekend heroes. *Ray Ryan*

from a single-downtube to dual-downtube design and, in the process, redesigned both the front forks and rear shocks. If you wanted changes, Honda had responded accordingly, and the 1980 model delivered enough to warrant a new price tag plus an extra ad campaign or two along the way. This then necessitated a rethink in the engine department, because the original port layout simply would not fit with a pair of downtubes cluttering the scenery.

Although porting changes were seemingly insignificant, the 1980 motor proved to be a grunter rather than a screamer, sending riders away to "short shift school" before they started winning races on their shiny new 80s.

In only two complete model years, Honda had salvaged the motocross reputation it had built so quickly and lost with equal rapidity. The company had gone from innovative market leader to a me-too performer and then bounced back with products that clearly reflected lessons learned from the real-world school of pro motocross.

Honda's changes to the basic CR250 concept beyond 1978 into the post-1980s ProLink era were evolutionary rather than revolutionary. They followed the same formula Honda had established with the CR250R: solid race bikes that could win Sunday races for weekend heroes, who would go home feeling like Marty Smith at the end of the day.

1978–80 Yamaha OW40

"A" Listed

The Staten bike used 1980 OW-spec 43mm fork tubes riding in fully machined upper and lower triple clamps. *Bill Forsyth*

Yamaha's production YZ250F didn't make many enemies when it appeared in 1978. In fact, most magazine testers loved the F. One magazine, *Cycle,* even went so far as to suggest that "only one rider in a million could ask for a better machine." The production YZ250F even earned its stripes in Pro-class Supercross, when U.S. Yamaha Team rider Mike Bell took his stock YZ250F to first place over teammate Bob Hannah at the Superbowl of Motocross in Los Angeles that year.

While the YZF's race potential kept the tills ringing at Yamaha shops, the bike that was taking Yamaha's team riders to victory bore little resemblance to any production YZ. Introduced in 1978 and raced over a three-year-evolution lifespan until 1980, the 250cc OW40, each of which was rumored to have cost over US$50,000, was Yamaha's last non– "Power Valve" design.

With the OW40's debut, Yamaha shifted the goalposts overnight. Its engineers had delivered a purpose-built, victory-focused weapon, a motocross machine devoid of any shared components with the production YZs and ringing the scales at around 202 pounds—almost 30 less than a 1978 YZ250F. Comparisons between any YZ and OW were pointless, particularly because the OW engine was designed from the ground up with features such as sand-cast magnesium cases and covers, a chrome-bore cylinder with a unique cylinder head pattern, and a center-port exhaust.

20

This ex–Rex Staten OW40 is now part of a private works bike collection in California. *Bill Forsyth*

The year 1978 had been strong for Yamaha, and the OW40 had already proven its potential with Bob Hannah's dominance of the 1978 U.S. Supercross series and Trans-AMA. Factor in Broc Glover's invincibility in the 125cc class and Heikki Mikkola's second-in-a-row 500cc World Championship title and Yamaha was clearly brimming with confidence. Its OW40 was a proven and competitive package, aimed squarely at U.S.-style stadium racing and its demands for lightning-fast engine response and flawless suspension.

Refinement and evolution of the existing OW40 design was the strategy Yamaha pursued for the 1979 season. Just two years earlier, Yamaha's 1977 OW25E predecessor, which was lighter still, was markedly similar to a production YZ in front forks and rear monoshock, along with other detail touches. Hardcore one-off trickery came of age with the OW40, with its fully machined front forks, carbon-fiber engine mounts and lever perches, braced

aluminum swingarm, fabricated aluminum rear brake pedal, and billet-style remote reservoir monoshock. Even the chain guide was machined from solid aluminum stock—a clear indication of Yamaha's total commitment to motocross supremacy.

Ironically, the OW40 lacked some minor refinements of earlier Yamaha factory bikes, thereby partially accounting for the weight differences. This included the demise of some titanium fasteners to make way for conventional steel or aluminum, but Yamaha responded by drilling anything that moved until it looked like metallic Swiss cheese. Foot pegs, axles, the swingarm pivot bolt, and even the foot-peg mounting bolts were all ventilated.

The forged-titanium kickstarter was both hi-tech and high budget, and the OW's hand-formed aluminum fuel tank also spelled big bucks. Even seemingly minor components were designed to minimize weight: a titanium swingarm pivot bolt, light-bodied Mikuni carb with a drilled slide and aluminum screws, a hand-formed, one-piece fiberglass airbox, and wafer-thin, lightweight polyethylene side covers.

Even allowing for production variances throughout any one model year, not all OWs were created equal—particularly as Yamaha shipped its OWs to the U.S. minus some of the finishing-touch add-ons, which were then completed to each team rider's preferences. Variations in seats, foot-peg heights, and handlebars were usually left to the rider, so that tall Mike Bell's OW40 used foot-pegs lower than those of Bob Hannah's. Other Yamaha riders, including Rick Burgett and Rex Staten, also had their personal setups.

Bob Hannah's 1979 model clearly demonstrates the individuality of Yamaha's team OWs and also gives some insight to the pecking order of the day. Hannah's 1979 OW40 is now owned by Chicago-based collector Terry Good. It weighs 196 pounds, with features such as magnesium fork legs and titanium fasteners throughout. Other OWs more closely followed the standard recipe, including the use of 37mm-diameter forks in 1979, before Yamaha uprated to 43mm units in 1980. One OW uprated to this

1980 specification was the bike Rex Staten rode to win the 1980 Daytona Supercross. This win marked Yamaha's last Daytona victory for an 18-year period, until Jeremy McGrath broke the curse in 1998.

The forks were pure machinist's art. Staten's bike used 1980 OW-spec 43mm fork tubes riding in fully machined upper and lower triple clamps. Their upper tubes were knurled at their contact points with the magnesium triple clamps, while the lower legs were so thoroughly machined that it was difficult to ascertain whether they were cast or turned from stock.

The same minimalist philosophy was apparent in the factory monoshock unit, which was markedly shorter than any production YZ unit of the time and carried external adjusters for damping as well as spring preload, along with a remote reservoir. A triple-rate spring was fitted with a thermostatically controlled oil-damping valve, which closed as the shock unit began to heat up. This reduced the damping fade normally caused by thinning oil.

In the hands of riders such as Hannah and Staten, the OW's twin-leading-shoe front brake proved to be Yamaha's secret weapon. Not an oversized, downscaled version of a street bike unit, the OW brake retained the compactness and characteristic look of the YZ front hub but, with a powerful twin-leading-shoe configuration, gave exceptional stopping power. While Suzuki's works-bike brakes grew in size and weight, Yamaha kept the OW40's critical unsprung weight on a strict diet.

OW40s are as much prized today as they ever were at the height of their professional motocross careers. While the survival ratio is high, OWs were never sold to the general racing public, and "name" bikes such as those once ridden by Hannah, Bell, or Staten occasionally change ownership within a small network of wealthy and dedicated collectors. Mike Bell's 1980 U.S. Supercross Championship OW40 was restored and is occasionally raced by one enthusiast in California. When he offered it for sale in 2001, the asking price was US$20,000!

One of Rex Staten's 1980 OW40s survives in another private collection, as does Rocket Rex's historic 1980

Daytona winner. The race patina of the Daytona-winner was faithfully preserved by a previous owner, who still prizes the OW for its "raw, aggressive beauty and the role it played in Staten's racing career."

He says, "Daytona 1980 was Rex Staten's first Supercross win at a time when Staten was a factory rider primarily in the 500 class. On that midsummer race day, Yamaha's heir-apparent Supercross Champion, Mike Bell, was dicing with Kent Howerton (Suzuki) and Chuck Sun (Honda) for the national title. Rex's team orders were to try to delay Kent Howerton and allow Bell to build up a lead around which he could extend his championship points standing.

"Unofficially, had Bell challenged Staten then, Rex would probably have felt obliged to let him pass. However, when the gate dropped, "Rocket Rex" lived up to his nickname and found himself in front of forty other top-line racers. Taking the lead, he forgot his team orders and went on to blitz the field in what was then the most prestigious event of the series next to the Superbowl of Motocross."

This unrestored OW, in pristine and original condition, carries its few dueling scars with pride—right down to the scrutineering stickers applied under the glaring Florida sun over 20 years ago.

Mike Bell's 1980 U.S. Supercross Championship OW40 was restored and is occasionally raced by a California enthusiast. *Bill Forsyth*

Stephen Gall's OW51 Yamaha

Transitional Technology

The OW51 had little in common with its YZ465G and H production counterparts. The magnesium sand-cast engine displaced almost 500cc and used a power valve developed through Yamaha's road-racing program. *Bill Forsyth*

Nineteen seventy-nine was a watershed year for Yamaha, one that marked a transition from the glory days of Heikki Mikkola's back-to-back World 500 titles in the two previous years to a lackluster fifth spot. Mikkola's midseason injuries had eliminated him from one GP round, but not even his legendary ferocious pace could help make up lost ground as the '79 season ticked away. By the final tally, Mikkola was out of the top three and announced his retirement with a total of five World Championship titles to his credit.

The decade had been kind to Yamaha. The company rode the top of the dirt bike sales charts in the U.S.A. and was consistently rated highly by the critical motorcycle press. Even though competition for motocross sales was tough, Yamaha remained cool and confident and seemed committed in its belief that GP wins made for highly saleable consumer-model race bikes.

In spite of such apparent corporate confidence, 1980 soon proved to be a less than brilliant year for Yamaha on the World GP stage. Hakan Carlqvist's arrival in the Yamaha camp was timely, but "Carla" could still notch up only a third place in his debut year on the white-and-red OW works bikes.

Out in the world of weekend motocross, Yamaha's YZ465G Open-class customer bike fared considerably better and quickly earned a reputation as the best weapon in that class. Its power was matched only by that of the 440

21

The OW51 helped raise the stakes in Australian motocross. *Bill Forsyth*

The OW51 was rumored to be heavier than the 231-pound YZ465H production model. *Bill Forsyth*

Maico, but the YZ was more user-friendly and versatile. Average riders loved the YZ465, and above-average riders used it to regularly win races.

On the Australian scene, Yamaha continued its winning ways in the prestigious Mister Motocross series, with Sydney racer Stephen Gall notching up his second Mister Motocross title on a production Yamaha motocrosser. In its seventh year, the 1980 series had culminated in a shootout at Amaroo Park, near Sydney, between Gall on the YZ465 and Trevor Williams on a works 440 Kawasaki. The stakes were being raised in Australian Pro-level motocross, and Williams' works Kawasaki was simply the top card on a fresh deck that would be played throughout the decade to come. Highly proficient production bikes such as the Yamaha YZ465 were no longer good enough to win at a professional level.

Yamaha intended to take no chances with Stephen Gall in 1981. They promptly landed a factory-fresh OW51 for the 23-year-old racer when he returned from the U.S.A. after a three-month racing break before the Australian season opened. With two Mister Motocross titles already under his belt, Gall was hot property for Yamaha and was undeniably the most promotable package in Aussie motocross.

In the time-honored tradition of Yamaha factory bikes, the OW51 had little in common with its production counterparts, the YZ465G and H models. For starters, the magnesium sand-cast engine displaced almost 500cc—a hefty punch in capacity from the production 465 that had already been crowned as the horsepower king. A four-speed gearbox was deemed sufficient to handle the massive torque. It also eliminated any problems potentially inherited from the five-speed that had proved troublesome on the 1980 production YZs.

Yamaha pulled no punches to ensure that the OW51 had the broadest possible powerband. The big bore was just a starting point for an engine that also packed Yamaha's new YEIS, or Yamaha Energy Induction System—a "boost bottle" by any other name. YEIS had already been used on Yamaha's GP machines, making its debut in 1980 on works water-cooled 125s campaigned by Marc Velkeneers and Tetsumi Mitsuyasu.

The system comprised a compact bottle connected to the carburetor/reed-valve junction by a piece of hose. It effectively eliminated any backflow of inlet gases into the carburetor body, giving Yamaha's conventionally reed-valved engines characteristics similar to those of case reed designs such as Suzuki's. A power valve was also included. Based on designs evolved through Yamaha's road-racing program, the mechanically controlled system varied the height of the exhaust port with engine speed.

Overall, the OW51 engine was a dynamite package, bristling with features that would eventually become production YZ components. The air-cooled OW engine was even equipped with the facilities to use an optional water-cooled barrel!

Although a European spec bike, the Gall OW51 arrived with a second seat and a smaller alloy fuel tank intended primarily for the U.S. race scene. Equally distinctive were the massive, full-width magnesium hubs, rather than the svelte, production-like YZ-style conical units Yamaha had long favored. Gall said at the time that U.S. Yamaha riders swapped their OWs to conical-style hubs before they even test-rode them.

The OW51 was rumored to be heavier than the 231-pound YZ465H. Today, Gall concedes that it was certainly no lightweight. "Weight was not really a factor with the OW," he recalls. "The bike had an engine that was an absolute killer, and that was the greatest part of the whole machine."

Strangely, despite its reputedly advanced monoshock, the OW left a lot to be desired in the handling department. "It just didn't handle as well as a production YZ, particularly in the rear end," Gall adds. "Sure, it turned easier, and the forks were better than the production units, but we actually went to a Fox monoshock on the OW in the hope that we could improve the rear end."

Gall laments that the OW51 was the last in a long line of traditional monoshock designs and that the model really only survived for half a season before it was replaced by the more advanced YZM500, with its linkage suspension. "We never saw any upgrades on the OW51, and the YZM was virtually an identical bike, only with the rising-rate rear suspension system."

Gall fired the opening salvo for Yamaha in the 1981 Mister Motocross series at Broadford, Victoria, in late May. The young Sydneysider was at his riding peak and took out round one of the national series, even after stalling the OW51 and reverting to a production YZ465.

After a brilliant season, he went into the series final with enough points to guarantee his third Mister Motocross title at its spiritual home track, Amaroo Park. Gall settled for nothing short of total domination of the Amaroo Park final, even though his title was already in the bag. Refusing to back off, he ground down all opposition with three heat wins out of four. The OW51 had been the big

gun in Gall's arsenal for his third, most memorable, and final Mister Motocross title.

As the 1982 race season unfolded, motocross design moved into the linkage suspension era, and the bike that had taken Gall to his ultimate Mister Motocross victory was soon forgotten. It languished in Gall's workshop for years before being salvaged by an avid collector of works motocross bikes, who gently persuaded Gall to allow him to resurrect the historic machine.

Today, Gall candidly remarks, "Perhaps it should have been destroyed or sent to the crusher . . . who knows? . . . What really matters is that it has survived and now represents the transition from Yamaha's original monoshock concept through to a new age of linkage suspension."

"Weight was not really a factor with the OW," Stephen recalls. "The engine was an absolute killer, and that was the greatest part of the whole machine." *Bill Forsyth*

PART III

The 1980s

Johnny O'Mara's 1980 Mugen 125W1

Star of the Show

Everything was hand built except the bottom end of the motor. Mugen craftsmanship was superb. *Bill Forsyth*

Mugen Company Limited, based in Saitama, Japan, was started in 1973 by Hirotoshi (Hiro) Honda, son of Soichiro Honda, founder of the Honda Motor Company. Its first creation was the Honda Civic–based FJ1300 Formula racing car engine, the MF 318. Within 12 months, the Mugen MF 318 engine dominated Japan's budding Formula 1300 open-wheel class, sparking Mugen's expansion into aftermarket auto tuning equipment, primarily for the Honda Civic.

Mugen's entry into motocross came in 1976, with a Honda CR250–based Mugen ME250 taking first place in the All Japan Motocross GP that year. The following year, Mugen released its own limited-production Honda-based bikes, the Mugen Special Complete Motocross, in ME125 and ME250 variants. Production began on the ME360 in 1978, and Mugen advanced to its second-generation ME125RZ and ME250RZ air-cooled models in 1979 before setting up a satellite U.S. operation in August that year. Based in Hesperia, near San Bernardino, California, Mugen U.S.A. Company Limited was headed up by Baja racer and businessman Al Baker. In November that year, Mugen and its newly signed team rider, 18-year-old Johnny O'Mara from Van Nuys, California, made national motorcycle news with their domination of the 125cc Supercross at Anaheim.

Mugen upped the R&D stakes immediately, releasing the water-cooled ME125W1 in January 1980 and then

22

Even with limited resources, impeccable preparation and attention to detail were the winning elements of Johnny O'Mara's Mugen 125s. *Bill Forsyth*

Before signing with Mugen, Johnny O'Mara had won three Southern California #1 plates—a total of 76 races in 1978 and 68 races in 1979.
Bill Forsyth

proving its clout with a first place in the Finland 125cc World Championship GP just months later. Johnny O'Mara, by this time labelled "Johnny O" by race fans and motorcycle press alike, stole the thunder from the world's best 125 riders with first and third place moto wins in the Valvoline 125cc USGP at Lexington, Ohio. The headline in *Cycle News* read "The Johnny O Show."

O'Mara and the water-cooled Mugen ME125W1 were a class act to behold in the crankcase-deep Ohio gloop as they slithered and powered their way ahead of European contenders such as Gaston Rahier, Eric Geboers, Dario Nani, Harry Everts, and Michele Rinaldi, along with fellow Americans Mark Barnett, Broc Glover, Tom Benolkin, Jeff Ward, and Ron Sun.

In doing so, O'Mara's Mugen obliterated the most exotic 125cc-class field ever assembled in the U.S., including works entries from Gilera, Yamaha, Honda, Suzuki, and TGM and the sole Kawasaki factory entry of Jeff Ward. O'Mara marked his first GP ride with outright victory after a knockdown duel with Suzuki's Mark Barnett that saw Barnett relinquish his lead to O'Mara just two laps from the finish of the first moto.

Impeccable preparation and attention to detail were the winning elements of The Johnny O Show wherever it played. Behind the scenes was no megadollar factory support or set dressing, just the limited resources of a few individuals who were as committed as Hiro and O'Mara to putting the Mugen name up front.

Tom Halverson was not only Johnny O'Mara's friend but also his longtime mechanic. Halverson worked with Mugen U.S.A. Company Limited's Al Baker and, along with former *Motocross Action* editor, Dick Miller, was instrumental in negotiating a sponsorship deal for Johnny with Hiro Honda. He recalls how Johnny's talent and commitment motivated and inspired the Mugen team.

"Before this point, Johnny had earned three Southern California number one plates, won 76 races in 1978 and 68 races in 1979. Mugen contracted us both in January of 1980, and Hiro-san gave explicit instructions on the look of the bike, the look of the rider, the truck . . . everything. From the clean original look down to the boot covers and font used for the 'Johnny O' on the seat, it was all his.

"The first bike Johnny rode was an air-cooled Mugen ME125RZ Super Pro Kit CR125. Along with the Super Pro Kit, that included a Mugen hard-chrome works alloy cylinder, cylinder head, piston, rings, gaskets, and clutch springs. That bike also had the Mugen frame, aluminum swingarm, and Showa racing suspension. Johnny's first win on the Mugen was in November of 1979, in the AME 125 Pro Class at Indian Dunes. His next was even bigger, in Anaheim Stadium in December of 1979, when he won the 125 Stadium Championship on this bike.

"The next kit was the Mugen Works Water Cooled ME125 W1 Banzai Kit for the air-cooled 1980 Honda CR125. It boasted very good cooling, low frictional losses, explosive power, and a fantastic torque boost in midrange. There was increased horsepower at top rpm. This kit included the water-cooled hard-chrome cylinder, the head, and a clutch cover which housed the water pump that fed the single radiator that mounted behind the vented front number plate. We built one at the shop, and Johnny rode it very little, as soon after, the bike we had been waiting for arrived—the YA1C.

"This bike was so trick for the time. The tank was crafted so that there was room to vent air through the twin radiators that mounted on the frame instead of the triple clamps. On the sides of the radiators were shrouds that were adjustable in length to closely control the water temperature of the engine. The craftsmanship on all the parts was top notch. It was light, fast, and handled great, with little similarity to the CR125 of that year. There was no comparison in handling—or performance, either."

O'Mara had a reputation as a perfectionist and a never-say-die rider who could rise above anything a motocross track or a fellow rider could throw his way. Tom Halverson cites Johnny's historic 125cc USGP win in Ohio: "Toughness and desire were the ingredients that brought Johnny that win. The mud was so incredible that goggles were useless, and I was in shock at the amount of mud we had to dig out of his eye sockets with Q Tips after the race.

"Johnny is one of the most fiercely dedicated people I have ever met. His training regime was incredible, and he cared very little about anything but achieving his goals of becoming a motocross champion. I gladly spent ten to twelve hours a day or more at his house, making sure his bike was perfect as well. Our whole operation was based out of his one-car detached garage that sat outside of his parents' humble Valley house. The box van I drove served as the parts room, and the garage served as the workshop and tire storage. That nineteen-year-old unknown kid from the Valley was the third American in a row to win a USGP."

Johnny went on to become a 125cc National and SX champion in 1983 and 1984. He also represented the U.S.A. in the MX des Nations on 125cc, 250cc, and Open-class machinery, and his performances indicated that he could have mixed it with the best on the 125cc GP world circuit. He showed his ultimate form in 1986 when he took his Honda 125 from the second row of the grid in the 1986 MXdN at Maggiora in Northern Italy and blitzed reigning 500cc world champion David Thorpe in the second moto.

In recent years, Johnny has worked with his former sponsor, Oakley, and as behind-the-scenes trainer for reigning U.S. champion Ricky Carmichael. Is it any surprise that Johnny O'Mara predicted back in 1998, "Ricky is going to be a hero to a new generation"?

1980 Suzuki RM250T and RM400T

Move Over, Maico

The RM250T quickly earned the nickname "The Money Machine," because a pro could buy the bike, race it in stock form, and win.
Bill Forsyth

It didn't take long for Suzuki's A-series RMs to be applauded as Japan's best production motocrossers when they hit the marketplace in 1975. Both the RM250A and its larger-engined brother, the RM370A, translated much of Suzuki's GP thinking into genuine production models for the first time ever. Just 12 months later, Suzuki again elevated its own race bikes and lifted the game of the entire motocross world in the process. The RM250B and RM370B that arrived in 1976 were clearly superior to even the first-wave RMs that had finally sealed the fate of the dismal TM range.

Outstanding was the new RM250B, with its previously buzzy engine now altered to a more torquey, longer-stroke 67mm x 70mm configuration. It was the starting point for a second generation of Suzuki RM powerplants that evolved through the first C models in 1977 to the radically revamped, but short-lived, RM-C2 series of 1978.

Unlike the 1977 RMs, which had been little more than a cosmetic makeover, the C2 was directly inspired by Suzuki's RH and RN works bikes. While the beautiful but delicate alloy fuel tank had been replaced by a more practical and less stylish yellow plastic item, the C2 was a major step forward in all aspects of engine and suspension performance. An exotic, extruded-aluminum swingarm was the most apparent change. Not only was it fractionally lighter than the previous chrome-moly type, it also provided greater rigidity.

23

The RM250 was right up there with the best. Weighing 237 pounds, it still managed to feel like a 125 to many riders. *Bill Forsyth*

This modified RM400T was built by Mike Tolle of Riverside, California.
Bill Forsyth

Straight out of the crate, the bike was a winner. Although the N model was visually similar to the RM-C, it was in fact a totally new design, with the steering-head angle trimmed from 30 degrees to 29 degrees to sharpen steering response. In turn, this shortened the wheelbase by around 1 inch, further improving the turn-in ability of the new T models.

Suzuki riders now compare the RM cornering technique to that of a Husky. The bike responds favorably when the rider leans over the tank to load the front wheel and uses the lip of a berm to hold a tight cornering line and get maximum drive on the exit. It translated the old theory "The more time a bike spends vertical, the more drive it gets" into race-winning reality.

Suzuki also addressed the early RM-series problem of excessive distance between the countershaft and the swingarm pivot and the consequent need for bulky and ineffective chain tensioners. By repositioning the N model's countershaft closer to the pivot point of the swingarm, it not only was similar to a Maico but needed only a simple, unsprung rubber chain guide.

Upgrading the lightweight swingarm to a new extruded box-section type fitted with needle rollers was the final refinement, along with shocks inclined at a more severe angle. Suzuki also relocated the foot pegs 1 inch higher than on the C model.

Even greater improvements lay within the new N model's 250 motor. While the new RM250N motor retained the familiar 67x70mm stroke configuration of the RM250B model, virtually everything beyond the crank was either changed or modified. Response throughout the entire power range was boosted by swapping the reed block from a two-petal steel reed to a three-petal fiber version. And whereas the C had two Siamese transfer ports, the N featured six individual transfers and a single, oval-shaped exhaust port that replaced the C's bridged exhaust port.

The engine had a new single-ring piston and a revised exhaust system, which still shared the expansion-chamber dimensions of the RM-C. Its CDI ignition was

This was combined with 20mm-longer Kayaba shocks that offered two-stage rebound damping adjustment plus an added 10mm of actual stroke. The only significant change required to the chassis was the relocation of the top shock mounting point to allow for the longer shock length without increasing seat height.

Subtle improvements also refined the front suspension, which maintained its 9.8 inches of travel yet featured revised rebound damping, increased oil capacity, and higher air-pressure settings.

The RMC2's short lifespan was no reflection on its abilities. Even while the C series was being released, Suzuki's R&D department had a totally new RM ready in the wings. In 1979, after 22 months of development, they unveiled the innovative RM-N.

upgraded to a new black box, producing a wider power spread. One novel approach to tuning was that Suzuki offered base gaskets of three different thicknesses, allowing the owner to raise or lower inlet timing without resorting to porting modifications. Suzuki also retained the RM250C's excellent transmission but replaced the antiquated rack-and-pinion clutch activation with a simpler internal push-rod design.

Right out of the crate, the RM250N was up there with the best. Weighing in at 237 pounds dry, the RM250N was no anorexic, yet the bike felt like a 125 to most riders. Other comments were equally positive, with comparisons even drawn to Maico. Times were changing. Now Suzuki was very much in control of the future of motocross.

The RM's gear selection was still one of the best, with neutral easy to find even when revving the bike. The larger RM400N was a cinch to start, even though it did not use the primary kick design of the RM125N and RM250N.

Braking performance was equally good, with a 130mm front brake and a rear that didn't lock up. In every way, the RM-N was a milestone design for Suzuki in both 250 and 400 models. It was so good, in fact, that the RM-T that followed in 1980 needed few changes to stay seriously competitive.

The RM-T appeared virtually identical to the N, except for a slightly larger fuel tank, reshaped mudguards, minor bracketing and cable routing changes, and the only major change: a 20mm-larger front brake. The engine and suspension remained the same solid package, and for good reasons.

While the 1980 RM400T was destined to compete for sales as well as race wins against Open-class weapons such as the 490 Maico and YZ400 Yamaha, it was once again Suzuki's smaller 250 model that had the big reputation. To many U.S. racers, the RM250T quickly earned the nickname "The Money Machine," because a pro could buy the bike, race it in stock form, and win. By comparison, the standard RM400T was more attuned to a less skilled racer who could make the most of the Suzuki's sweet handling without being disadvantaged by its lack of muscle against

the Maico or YZ. That both the RM250T and RM400T are still frequently referred to as "Japanese Maicos" is the greatest compliment that can be paid to Suzuki's ultimate twin-shock RM racers.

But not even the N's survival in born-again guise could hold back Suzuki's need to evolve its most effective ever motocross design. Within a year of the T model's release, Suzuki introduced the now legendary X model, with its revolutionary single-shock, linkage rear end. It made anything with twin-shock suspension obsolete overnight, including Suzuki's own earlier RMs.

Some of the greatest bikes of the late 1970s and early 1980s were the Suzuki RM250 and 400.

1980 Yamaha YZ465G

Mister Muscle

When Open-class motocross bikes go horribly wrong, their shortcomings are painfully obvious to the racers left to limp away from the wreckage. So with its fair share of earlier Open-class horrors buried in the corporate vaults, Yamaha engineers might have been feeling optimistic yet cautious when they unveiled their 1980 YZ465G.

Yamaha's 1980 range marked the third evolutionary upgrade of the patented "Monocross" single-shock suspension system. Introduced with the limited-production YZ250B and YZ360B in 1974, Yamaha's monoshock initially delivered a quantum performance and marketing advantage. Within 12 months, Yamaha packaged the monoshock with its volume-production YZ125C, MX250B, and MX400B models.

That first-generation monoshock remained unchanged throughout the subsequent YZ250C and YZ400C, but advances in conventional twin-shock LTR designs through new gas/oil shock-absorber technology were already beginning to erode Yamaha's strong position.

Within just a few years, motocross suspension design had become a science, forcing Yamaha to revise the original Tilkiens-concept monoshock with the YZD series in 1977. The new, more compact unit eliminated the need for a bulky separate nitrogen reservoir and was more easily set up to suit an individual rider's preferences. Both compression and rebound damping could be adjusted with the new monoshock still in place on the bike.

1n 1978, with the YZE range, Yamaha introduced longer and more rigid aluminum swingarms to complement

24

With its revised porting, rejetted 38mm Mikuni carb, redesigned exhaust, and a new CDI ignition system, the YZ465H ranked as the best 500cc-class racer from Japan. *Bill Forsyth*

the uprated monoshock. As well as trimming around 2 pounds from each of its three prime YZ models, the alloy arms added almost an extra inch to the YZ's wheelbase.

By its third model year, the YZ400 was reaping the rewards of evolution, with the YZ400E quietly slipping into the unofficial role of King of the Dirt. Although the 400 delivered around 40 horsepower, its basic engine had remained virtually unchanged since its inception.

By 1979, a major revamp was essential for the continuing success of the biggest YZ. With the launch of the YZ400F, Yamaha marked a new direction in its Open-class engine design, shifting away from the early short-stroke configuration to a torquier long-stroke (75mm) design with a smaller, 82mm bore. Capacity was just under 400cc. Combined with major porting and exhaust system changes, a larger reed-valve assembly, and heavier flywheels, the YZ400F proved to be the tractor Yamaha's design team had hoped for.

In every respect, the 1979 YZ400F was the force to be reckoned with in Open-class motocross, yet not even that prestige could insulate Yamaha from the need to be constantly on top of emerging suspension technology. Although brilliant at the time of its inception, Yamaha's monoshock was showing its age by the end of the seventies. Even the second-generation design was still prone to overheating and suffered the legacy of high unsprung weight.

In 1980, Yamaha tackled the monoshock's woes head on with a fresh third-generation layout. This dispensed with the heavy backbone tunnel of earlier designs and mounted the exposed and inverted single shock direct to the upper frame tubes. A remote oil reservoir was introduced to reduce fade, and rear-wheel travel finally reached the 12-inch limit riders had once thought was mere fantasy. It could not have been a better time for Yamaha to up the ante in the Open class, quietly shelving the already much-improved YZ400 engine in favor of an even more deadly weapon: the YZ465G.

With the introduction of the YZ465G in 1980, Yamaha moved from a 400cc Open-class motor to 465cc.

This larger engine was achieved by increasing both bore and stroke and was part of a total revamp that also saw the introduction of narrower crankcases and a smoother-shifting, beefed-up transmission package that no longer used undercut gears.

If the motor and chassis were winners, Yamaha also left little to chance in the braking department, finally burying the almost vintage single-leading-shoe conical front brake in use for almost a decade. The new twin-leading- shoe (TLS) front brake introduced the following year on the YZ465H was visually similar to the original YZ unit but delivered massive stopping power. Right up until the introduction of disc brakes, the TLS Yamaha unit remained an industry standard, with its light touch, precise feedback, and progressive action.

The YZ465 quickly earned a reputation as being more than just a powerhouse. Wrapped in a long-wheel-base, third-generation monoshock chassis, it combined a rider-friendly broad powerband, razor-sharp steering, and unprecedented stopping power along with the accepted Japanese design virtues of reliability and durability. To virtually every test rider who unleashed its muscle, not only was the YZ465G the best Japanese Open-class mo-tocross weapon of 1980, it even knocked the Maico 440M1 off its pedestal.

The YZ's ultimate elevation to the King of the Dirt throne was both timely and appropriate, yet it was destined to be short-lived. In 1981, Maico unleashed the leg-endary MC490. Yamaha responded with an improved and further-refined 465, the YZ465H. Although incapable of guarding the crown in the Open class, it still ranked as the best 500cc-class racer from Japan. Improvements included revised porting and the introduction of a rejetted 38mm Mikuni carb, along with a redesigned exhaust and a new CDI ignition system.

Although the YZ had quietly slipped from number one to second spot in the 1981 Open-class market, it gave away little to an opposition lineup comprising some of the best models ever. Even if the Suzuki RM465 now threatened Yamaha's domination, it still could not match the big YZ, with its broad powerband and superb low-end response.

Motocross buyers were finally calling the shots at all the factories, which responded unanimously with some of the most potent and competitive two-strokes ever to hit the berms. In addition to the Maico Mega Two 490 were other take-no-prisoners racers such as Honda's CR450, the "floater"-suspended RM465 Suzuki, and the Uni-Trak Kawasaki KX420. Representing the European camps, the KTM495, Husky 430CR, and CanAm 400 were almost as challenging. These bikes represented the pinnacle of Open-class, air-cooled technology—all ca-pable of delivering 40 horsepower or more, along with 12 inches of suspension travel from their sophisticated twin-shock or single-shock systems.

Whether Yamaha had begun to underestimate the weight of such opposition or was merely steamrolled by runaway technology is unknown. However, the minor changes the company introduced to the YZ490 from its debut G series to the final run H model in 1981 were in-sufficient. More radical changes were needed if Yamaha hoped to have any chance of once again being number one in the 500cc class. On paper, the YZ that followed in 1982 looked as though it might be Yamaha's much-needed Open-class messiah.

History would soon prove that the YZ490J, with its mammoth muscle, dubious four-speed transmission, and inadequate suspension, was not the Chosen One.

Unfortunately, Yamaha already knew from past expe-riences that when things go wrong with big-bore MXers, they are rarely rectified in a single model run.

Opposite: **The YZ delivered almost as much muscle as a 490 Maico and was Japan's horsepower king.** *Bill Forsyth*

1981 Kawasaki SR500

One Hundred Percent Attitude

The SR500's sand-cast, four-speed motor was based on the one Brad Lackey used in the 1980 500cc World Championship. *Bill Forsyth*

"Win on Sunday, sell on Monday" has proven a flawless formula for selling production motocross bikes. Edison Dye's early years in the U.S. with his Husqvarna entourage of Super Swedes, Marty Smith's Honda Red Devils, and Jim Pomeroy's historic 1973 GP win on a Bultaco Pursang are all part of MX history and proof of this theory. Each of the respective manufacturers reaped the benefits of increased sales through raising their motocross profile.

Kawasaki set out on a similar mission in Australia in 1981. Kawasaki Australia needed to capitalize on its international motocross reputation to boost local sales and brand loyalty. What was happening for Kawasaki in Europe and the U.S.A. was making little positive impact on the remote yet potentially lucrative Australian market. So when three Kawasaki works SR500s were imported in 1981, they were seen as evidence of the Australian distributor's commitment to dominate the booming motocross market.

When the bikes landed in Australia, their Grand Prix heritage was immediately obvious. With a full 500cc displacement, their air-cooled engines were emblazoned "GP" on the alternator cover and "KX500" on the clutch cover. Blue-painted frames and engines and integral side number plates molded into the rear guards made them instantly distinguishable from production KX racers. Virtually all unpainted or alloy surfaces, such as the swingarm, rims, triple clamps, fork sliders, rear shock reservoir, chain guide, and rear-brake torque arms, were anodized gold.

25

The SR500 weighed around 209 pounds—at least 11 pounds less than a production-model KX. *Bill Forsyth*

The arrival of Team Kawasaki Australia SR500s in early 1981 instantly upped the stakes in pro motocross. *Bill Forsyth*

Two braided steel lines ran to a remote reservoir—one carried fluid up to the reservoir, and the other then returned the fluid to the shock body. This was a new concept at the time and was not repeated on later SR designs. The preload adjustment was at the top of the shock—the opposite of production Uni-Traks.

In Australia, the Kawasaki works shock was used and created constant problems. Team Kawasaki Australia rider Trevor Williams had suffered three shock failures and had also heard of similar breakages in Europe. With each shock costing thousands of dollars, often more than the cost of a single production KX, these failures were seriously impacting Kawasaki's budget. It didn't take long for Kawasaki to respond by flying an engineering team out to Australia. Williams remembers that during a meeting, one of the Japanese engineers reached into his bag and produced not one but three brand-new shocks of an improved design! Once these were fitted, Williams' SR suspension woes were over.

Up front, the SR's 43mm-diameter forks featured featherweight billet magnesium sliders mounted in gold-anodized billet-aluminum triple clamps. Compression damping could be easily tuned by means of an adjuster in the bottom of the slider.

At the heart of the SR500 was a sand-cast four-speed motor, based closely on the one used by Brad Lackey to finish second in the 1980 World 500cc Championship. Even though Lackey narrowly missed the World Championship title that year, 1980 was still a landmark year for Kawasaki, coinciding with the introduction of water cooling on their smaller 125cc factory bikes. Kawasaki had made it clear that liquid cooling was a sign of the future, and by 1982 its works KX250SRs were also walking on water. This left only its Open-class 500 bikes to await 1983 and the arrival of Georges Jobe and the first of the non-air-cooled works KX500s.

As the ultimate development of Kawasaki's big-bore, air-cooled designs, the SR500 was refined and easily adapted to riders' styles and the demands of individual motocross tracks. The configuration of the motor allowed

Each SR500 weighed in at around 209 pounds—a weight saving of at least 11 pounds over a stock KX. Straight from the GP tracks of Europe were the hydraulic front disc brake and a handmade alloy fuel tank—the crowning touches for such exotic, hard-hitting weapons.

Beneath the SR's macho looks was flawless engineering detail. Motocross was the perfect medium for Kawasaki to strut its technology, and the 1981 SR500 was no modest understatement. Kawasaki's Uni-Trak rear suspension first appeared in 1980, after being developed by U.S. works riders Brad Lackey, Jim Weinert, and Mickey Boone. Its unique falling-rate design used a special billet aluminum–bodied rear shock with a large, finned reservoir mounted on the left side of the frame, just below the rear mudguard.

the displacement to be varied from 460cc up to 499cc. The long-stroke 499cc setup could be reduced to 460cc by removing a spacer under the barrel and installing a different crankshaft with a longer stroke.

In addition, the powerband could be altered by rotating the ignition backing plate on the right side. This allowed the power delivery characteristics to be tuned for different tracks. A further ignition-related change was a twin-plug cylinder head fed by a coil with two high-tension leads to reduce detonation and improve combustion in the chamber.

Other details were equally well conceived, with the airbox a one-off, vacuum-formed unit in blue impregnated plastic and the intake area located high, just under the seat. A handmade cone exhaust pipe mated to a repackable aluminum silencer completed the SR's unique, aggressive looks.

The front disc brake was Kawasaki's second attempt to adapt this road-based technology to its works bikes. The disc was mounted on a hand-turned aluminum billet hub, kept to an absolute minimum size to reduce weight. The first disc design that appeared on Kawasaki's factory bikes in 1980 mounted the caliper in front of the left fork leg. However, the shortcomings of this layout caused factory engineers to relocate the caliper to the rear of the fork leg on the 1981 works bikes and to incorporate a protective alloy cover. This fundamental design found its way onto 1982 Kawasaki's production bikes, and by 1983, all Japanese manufacturers had followed suit.

At first glance, the rear brake was a conventional-design drum, but it incorporated a hand-turned aluminum-billet hub. This was unusual at a time when hubs on nearly all bikes, works or production, were cast in either aluminum or magnesium. The brake backing plate was a sand-cast magnesium one-off, as was the gold-anodized brake actuator, milled from billet to slot into the tiny space between the swingarm and the brake backing plate.

Even if the Gunnar Gasser throttle and KX grips and levers were production items, the SR's handlebars were a far cry from what could be found in any Kawasaki dealer. They used a special compound chrome-moly steel reputed to

have extra strength. Equally exotic was the handmade aluminum fuel tank that replaced the more fragile fiberglass versions used on the works bikes in 1980.

While the Team Kawasaki Australia SR500s enjoyed enormous success on the track, the unprecedented impact of these bikes was the interest they generated among race fans and press alike. The presence of genuine factory race bikes added a new dimension of excitement and atmosphere to Australian motocross.

1981 Maico MC490 Mega Two

Power of Seduction

The MC490 exemplified German minimalist engineering at its finest.
Bill Forsyth

Would-be racers were confronted by a mouthwatering range of alternatives in Open-class motocrossers in 1981. Freedom of choice had reached its zenith as riders were tempted by some of the fastest, hardest-hitting motocrossers ever created. Any buyer with $3,000 in his pocket could choose from the Honda CR450R, Husqvarna 430CR, KX420 Uni-Trak Kawasaki, KTM495, CanAm 400, or Suzuki linkage-suspension RM465. Yamaha's YZ465H was also prominent on this exclusive shopping list.

Even in the midst of this fast company, the talk always somehow turned to the bike that pushed desirability beyond temptation. Maico's new 490 Mega Two was not only the number one contender, it was also the bike used as a reference point by riders of all other brands. Whether a particular bike was fast or not was never the question. All that mattered was, "Will it beat a 490 Maico?"

Maicos had long been revered as great-handling machines, but for too many riders they were also notoriously unreliable. "Maico breako" was more than just a throwaway line—it summarized the problems an average Maico rider would endure in the hope of eventual victory. Maico's Bosch points-style ignitions were most often its downfall, along with vibration-induced frame cracks, engine air leaks, and Stone Age castings.

Maico Mayhem afflicted not only weekend racers but also 500cc World Championship contender Ake Jonsson

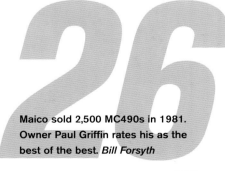

Maico sold 2,500 MC490s in 1981. Owner Paul Griffin rates his as the best of the best. *Bill Forsyth*

123

The 490 Maico was one of the most awesome motocross engines ever made, with around 53 horsepower at 7,000 rpm. *Bill Forsyth*

in 1972, when all he had to do was beat Roger DeCoster across the finish line in the season's final moto to win the coveted title. With Ake in the lead, the spark plug threads on his Maico's sand-cast head pulled out, the spark plug ejected, and Ake was left like so many other Maico riders, stranded trackside.

Fortunately, Maico's popular reputation was reinvented by the late seventies, enhanced by the company's high profile in European and U.S. Pro motocross. These were among the most progressive years in the history of motocross, and no factory could afford to rest on its laurels. In an environment of constant product development, even a motorcycle that was highly desirable one season could be bargain-binned the next if it failed to meet the demands, real or perceived, of motocross buyers.

Maico had stayed ahead in this constantly expanding marketplace, making the most of its European motocross heritage and rounding off the decade with one of its sweetest-handling race bikes, the 440cc Magnum in 1979. But not even the Magnum could promise security in such a competitive environment, so Maico entered the eighties with a new model: the 440cc Mega One. With its new Honda-style frame and ultra-long-travel 42mm-diameter forks, the Mega One appeared to be a natural progression from Maico's previous Magnum model and seemed destined to deliver Maico from its role as a second-level manufacturer.

Nothing could have been further from the truth. In its bid to stay ahead, Maico had changed too many things. Maico's engineers had thrown the baby out with the bathwater by radically altering the suspension geometry to create an ill-handling motocross mutant. The teetering Mega One also required a stepladder for riders under six feet tall.

Even Wheelsmith Engineering, Maico's de facto aftermarket guru in California was not impressed. Wheelsmith and the American Maico distributors both sent the same strong message to the German factory: Something had to be done quickly, or Maico sales would evaporate!

Maico's transformation of its Open-class racer from a lemon to a legend was rapid and definitive. Incorporating feedback from Wheelsmith and other dealers, the factory launched the 1981 Mega Two with a Magnum-style frame and shorter, 42mm forks. This new layout did not compromise suspension travel, and Maico's handling credentials were reinstated overnight. Despite some shortcomings as a total race weapon, the Magnum also provided the competitive and unbreakable 440cc engine that Maico then punched out to 490cc for its renaissance in the Mega Two.

There is no doubt that the 490 Maico was one of the most awesome motocross engines ever made. It produced staggering power, around 53 horsepower at 7,000 rpm, but was backed up by a user-friendly power curve teamed with flawless suspension.

Maico sold more 500-class bikes in 1981 than Honda sold over its entire motocross range, and even today, many pro riders still believe the 490 motor would be competitive against most new-millennium technology. Over 20 years later, it is almost as fast as a CR500 Honda or KTM525SX—even with air cooling, an agricultural Bing carb, and no reed valves or variable exhaust timing!

Yet the 490 was not without some faults, primarily the tragically inadequate Corte & Cosso shocks and forks, which were cursed with the usual Maico seal problems. It also had a feeble and mostly ornamental front brake, sand-cast cobby engine cases, and a clutch that used bent washers instead of coil springs. Still, the 490 was a masterpiece, because it exemplified German minimalist engineering at its finest.

These imperfections were only minor annoyances, for the Mega Two was seemingly perfect to everyone. Except, of course, to the wizards at Wheelsmith Engineering in California. They immediately set to work to make the perfect motocross bike even more so, with pipes that produced an even broader power spread, high-flow reed-valve conversions, fork revalving, and billet-aluminum components to replace the mild-steel production-line originals. While Wheelsmith didn't radically change the 490, they refined it to a point of almost-perfection rarely achieved since.

Despite the superb handling of the twin-shock Mega Two, market forces dictated that for any bike to be a sales success, it had to have single-shock rear suspension. What happened in 1982 and beyond makes the impact of the '81 Maico 490 even more significant.

High expectations surrounded the launch of Maico's '82 models, and racers had been promised a new rising-rate, Japanese-style linkage suspension with an Ohlins shock to further improve their advantage over the competition. The reality dawned as a linkage design that was flawed to begin with, coinciding with manufacturing deficiencies that only exacerbated the problem. Rear shock-absorber shafts were snapping in half on almost every bike.

On investigation, it was revealed that Maico's rear suspension had a 7:1 rocker arm ratio when rival Honda, with a similar setup, had a ratio of 1.6:1. While all of this was happening, rear hubs were also shattering at an alarming rate. Someone at the factory had gotten it terribly wrong. Maico dealers started fielding complaints from disgruntled customers, along with the odd lawsuit from injured riders.

Maico went back to the drawing board for 1983 with an all-new motor. It was so new that most of the components are still being used today. The problem was that the new motor, while more current in design, just didn't perform like the 490 of old. It revved to the moon but never seemed to make the horsepower or torque of the '81. The magic, for all intents and purposes, was gone.

More than 20 years after it was introduced, the MC490 is almost as fast as modern open-class bikes. This all the more remarkable considering the Maicio makes incredible power with air cooling, a simple Bing carb, and no reed valves or variable exhaust timing.
Bill Forsyth

1982-83 Honda CR480R

Open-Class Act

Altering the lever ratio on the Pro-Link and fitting a new rear shock eliminated the fade of the old CR450 Pro-Link setup. *Bill Forsyth*

In spite of its dominant market presence with the production Elsinore CR250M, Honda was not represented in Open-class motocross until late 1973. A one-off or prototype Open-class bike, believed to be in the region of 450cc and ridden by Honda's Gary Chaplin, made little impact on the flying Europeans who spearheaded the 1973 Trans-AMA field.

Beyond that point, Honda's Open-class aspirations were destined to lie dormant until 1975. With no big-bore production CR model available to the public, Honda's competition focus mirrored the realities of the marketplace. Honda's 125- and 250-class factory bikes helped sell production CR125s and CR250s. Open-class race bikes did not share this agenda.

Honda had also been slow to embrace new suspension technology, but LTR did finally impact the Japanese giant in 1975, when new all-red RC factory bikes were unveiled. Any lineage to a production Elsinore was visual at best, with the lineup comprising the RC125-75, RC250-75, and an Open-class contender, the RC400-75.

Throughout the season and beyond, Honda experimented with various engine configurations for its Open-class RCs. Bore, stroke, and capacities were all altered with the RCs racing in 360cc, 380cc, 400cc, 420cc, 460cc, and even 480cc trim. Honda's Pierre Karsmakers took his RC to third spot in the U.S. 500cc National Championships.

The following year, Honda reentered the Open class with even greater commitment evident in its RC400-76.

27

Honda styling was rarely cleaner than with the 1983 CR range. *Bill Forsyth*

For 1983, the CR480R front forks offered 14 stages of compression adjustment. *Bill Forsyth*

Its first production model 500cc-class motocrosser drew more criticism than it did praise. It was immediately obvious that the CR450R was a far cry from the RC works bikes from which Honda claimed to draw its lineage. Not even Honda's World 500–class domination by Andrew Malherbe for two consecutive seasons in 1980 and 1981 enhanced the desirability of the CR450R.

Nineteen eighty-two was destined to be the do-or-die year for Honda's biggest CR. With everything to gain and much-advertised input from Roger DeCoster, Honda revamped the imperfect CR450. The CR480R that emerged was more a new machine than an upgrade.

More powerful, more durable, and more refined in every way, the 480 quickly proved to be the bike the 450 should have been. In fact, many riders who bought one said this was exactly the bike Honda had claimed the old 450 to be—a user-friendly, Open-class racer that translated much of Honda's GP-winning expertise into a production motorcycle they could actually buy. Coming in more than 2 pounds lighter than its 450 predecessor, the 480 made the right impression from day one. It weighed 226 pounds, right on the button, and on par with the best of the era, including Yamaha's YZ465 hole-shot king.

The CR480R was competitive in price as well as specification and shattered any fables that "big Hondas don't work." Almost 30cc larger than its predecessor, the CR480R was predictably more powerful, but that alone did not give the new bike its edge. Honda had also redesigned the drivetrain, from the four-speed gearbox to the entire clutch assembly, but had wisely retained the gear ratios of the 450.

The larger motor delivered smoother, stronger power right across the board, but "more" was always the keyword. No matter how subtly it was phrased, the fact that the CR480R produced bucketfuls of power was never understated. It was, and remains today, a bike for the expert rider.

This one also had the suspension to match. Travel remained the same as the CR450, but Honda had uprated to 43mm-diameter forks, complete with three-way,

Karsmaker's bike featured an LTR Showa suspension package with around 11 inches of travel but delivered the expatriate Dutchman only two national 500-class wins throughout the year. Karsmakers jumped ship to Yamaha in '77, leaving his former Honda teammates Marty Smith and Tommy Croft to enjoy the fruits of his 1976 Open-class R&D. The RC400s they rode that year offered 12 inches of suspension travel but still bore no resemblance to any Honda production motocrosser.

Even as the factory RCs continued their successful evolution through the conquering RC450-78, Honda remained oblivious to calls from the marketplace for a production 500-class motorcycle.

By 1980, the company still lacked an Open-class contender, but the long-awaited Pro-Link CR450R was only 12 months away. Shortly after its debut, the CR450R sparked the news that Honda had never wanted to hear.

externally adjustable damping and scope for fine-tuning through air-pressure adjustment plus a range of optional springs. For once, Honda forks received more praise than criticism. It seemed the factory had also responded to feedback on the Pro-Link, altering the lever ratio and fitting a new rear shock to overcome the massive fade that had plagued the 450's Pro-Link setup.

Honda's corporate obsession with detail refinements also reached new levels with the CR480R. The bike bristled with lightweight, cast-alloy brackets, molded rubber insulator blocks, anti-vibration fittings, and featherweight 8mm alloy bolts. There was even an optional spares kit, which some dealers included free with the bike. It contained springs, gearing, oversize piston kits, gaskets, and Keihin jets.

Honda had finally jumped into the deep end, even though the company acknowledged "detailed use of Roger DeCoster's advice" in sorting out its shop-window race bike. Its efforts were well spent, and riders applauded the CR480 engine and suspension package with a level of enthusiasm no Honda big-bore had previously enjoyed. It was a hallmark motorcycle—at last—from the Japanese giant that had first defined production motocross design with its CR250M just ten years earlier.

Ergonomics, the elusive refinement of man-machine interface, had also driven Honda's designers with the CR480R and would now influence all future Honda moto-cross models.

Twelve months later, Honda may have been basking in the glory of the CR480's debut, but that did not deter the introduction of some refinements for its second model year in 1983. A five-speed gearbox headed the list, allowing the use of closer ratios throughout the cluster, along with the introduction of a CR250R-type clutch using pulp-style friction plates. The cylinder barrel and head fins were thickened, and Honda's front forks now offered 14 stages of compression adjustment.

Other refinements included the use of straight-spoke wheels, serrated-edge alloy wheel rims to eliminate tire creep, and a 23 percent boost in front-brake stopping

Winning on the CR demanded a confident, aggressive style. The tougher you treated it, the more the 480 loved you! *VMX Library—Geoff Eldridge, 1982*

power over the previous year's model. Seat height was also reduced, from 38.5 inches to 38, while Honda's dietitians also managed to shed another 2 pounds from the new racer. It now weighed just over 224 pounds, thanks to such aluminum goodies as the steering stem, rear brake arm, Pro-Link components, silencer, kickstart lever, and clutch plates. Magnesium was used for the front and rear brake shoes, brake hub plates, and clutch cover. It was Honda's lightest big-bore yet.

By 1984, the CR480R had been pushed into the background to make way for a bold new generation of water-cooled CRs. However, Honda's biggest CR was given a reprieve and was reborn yet again as the CR500R, with a 491cc air-cooled engine, front disc brake, and only minor additional changes. It weighed just 225 pounds.

The one Honda CR that would endure long enough to become an anachronism in the next millennium had clearly learned the great lesson of survival.

1983 Husqvarna 510

Swedish Bullet Train

The 510's conventional 40mm forks and a 28-degree steering head angle reflected the bike's role as either a motocrosser, desert racer or ISDE contender. *Bill Forsyth*

Twenty years later and lined up alongside a 2003 model Honda CRF450R, a 1983 Husqvarna 510TX might look a little pudgy. However, from an 1980s perspective, the Husky 510 was the lightest, toughest four-stroke of its era.

Husqvarna's off-road racing heritage was instantly apparent in the early 1980s, when Husky's new four-stroke motor first saw the light of day. Unlike the cooking-tune Honda XL/XR or Yamaha XT/TT engines, the air-cooled Husqvarna 510 four-stroke was a no-frills race motor, devoid of aspirations to a more sedentary dual-sport life.

Rather than play follow-the-leader with a bulky, Japanese-style SOHC air-cooled four-stroke, Husqvarna applied three key design criteria at the outset of its project: Husky's new engine had to be as light and slim as possible, with the lowest achievable center of gravity.

Husky engineers focused on low engine weight as the vital ingredient in creating a competitive off-road four-stroke. Logically, they approached the new four-stroke concept from a two-stroke perspective, drawing on their own experience as well as the basic engine configuration of existing two-stroke models. They had specified ultra-narrow crankcases, so many existing two-stroke engine components were used, some adapted to work in the alien environment of valves and camshafts.

In essence, the Husky team adapted an existing two-stroke design to accommodate the cam chain and valve gear drive needed for a four-stroke. If that in itself was not

28

Husqvarna created the 510 four-stroke using two-stroke priorities; their mission was to make the bike slim, compact and lightweight. *Bill Forsyth*

lateral thinking, they then abandoned the idea of using a conventional oil pump and specified a two-stroke–inspired mist lubrication system combined with a dry sump. Not only was the weight of an oil pump eliminated from the equation, but the dry sump also allowed a significant reduction in overall engine height.

Two-stroke design principles also influenced the choice of transmission, and the 510 gearbox was an existing Husky two-stroke design, produced in two variants: a close-ratio four-speed for the 510TC Motocross model and a six-speed cluster for the 510TE Enduro and 510TX Cross Country.

Such a compact powerplant also allowed Husky to use a slim two-stroke–style chassis in 4130 chrome-moly. The curved upper-frame backbone tube of the 510 was the only difference between it and the WR two-stroke chassis. As a result, the 510 weighed just 17.6 pounds more than the two-stroke Husky 500XC with which it shared most major components.

Absolute proof that "less is more," the 510 motor was pure simplicity. Available in two capacities (490cc and 503cc) and fitted to three models, its specifications read like an aftermarket tuning catalog: four-valve cylinder head, forged aluminum piston, chain-driven OHC configuration with the camshaft running in bearings, and rocker arms with roller-bearing followers.

A specially designed steel clutch basket was used to deposit huge amounts of oil onto the cam chain, which then delivered all top-end lubrication. Bottom-end lubrication was by an equally ingenious method that Husky termed Reed Activated Lubrication (RAL).

This system used the piston to function like an oil pump, so that when it moved upward in the cylinder it created a partial vacuum in the engine crankcase. At a specified point, the piston uncovered a port in the cylinder wall, and oil mist was drawn into the cylinder. This oil mist lubricated the moving parts and also allowed surplus oil to collect at the bottom of the crankcase. When the piston moved downward, pressure built up in the crankcase, and the surplus oil was expelled via a reed valve to the gearbox.

Without any need for an oil pump, Husky provided engine oil for heat transfer as well as lubrication.

Cold starting was not a problem, thanks to the pumper-style 36mm Dell'Orto carb and a manual valve lifter, provided a strict discipline of zero throttle was followed religiously. Hot starts were a far different story. Riders soon learned the drill of shutting off the fuel tap, kicking the motor over to clear away the remaining fuel, and then holding their mouths just the right way. If everything was done by the book, a dead 510 might just leap back to life like Lazarus with one kick.

To anyone expecting massive down-low grunt and a degree of docility, the 510 was an eyeopener. Unlike the more mundane big Japanese four-strokes, the 510 was a competition-oriented powerhouse, capable of mixing it with real-world two-stroke race bikes. Although not many test reports appeared on the 510, those few that made it to print unanimously ranked the Husky as the bullet train of the four-stroke world.

Fortunately, Husqvarna's design focus went well beyond the 510's brilliant engine. Other weight-saving factors were also at work to keep the 510TX down to a svelte 264 pounds, including dual mufflers, which were not just a styling touch but also trimmed weight and minimized bulk. To meet exhaust noise requirements with its dual-pipe exhaust system, Husky would have needed to install a single muffler that weighed nearly three times as much as its compact dual units.

In common with Husky's 1983 two-stroke models, the 510 used the twin-shock Ohlins ITC or Immediate Track Control (ITC) rear suspension system, which was as good as, if not better than, the new-breed single-shock designs of the day. All three 510 models used the twin-shock ITC layout and a 28-degree steering-head angle, which proved to be the best compromise for the 510's multifaceted role as motocrosser, desert racer, and ISDE contender.

Also common to all three models were conventional 40mm forks and powerful 6.3-inch twin-leading-shoe front brakes. Front suspension travel ranged from 10.6

Above: Chunky 5.00 x 18 four ply Trelleborg and non-floating rear brakes were used on all three 510 models. *Bill Forsyth*

inches for the 503cc six-speed 510TE Enduro to 11.8 inches on the 490cc four-speed 500TC Motocross and 503cc six-speed 510TX Cross Country. Rear wheel travel was 11.8 and 13.5 inches, respectively.

Potent as it was, the 510 proved to be less than perfect in its debut year and earned a reputation for burning pistons and melting ignitions. While Husky was unable to fully address the heating problems until it converted the 510 to liquid cooling in 1986, it did partially rectify the ignition meltdowns by relocating the ignition components up under the fuel tank in 1984. Unfortunately, throughout 1984 the air-cooled 510 engines continued to run hot, and the ignition still lost at least half its efficiency through overheating. Fuel vaporization problems were commonplace.

The 1986 arrival of liquid cooling gave the 510 a new lease on life. Dropping the operating temperature by around 86 degrees Fahrenheit instantly enhanced its reputation as the most powerful four-stroke in the business. It was now also as reliable as a rock and could be hot-started by mere mortals.

Opposite: The four-stroke 510 weighed just 17.6 pounds more than the two-stroke Husky 500XC. *Bill Forsyth*

1983–85 Kawasaki SR500

Steppingstones to Success

Georges Jobe won five World Championship titles, although none were for Kawasaki. *Bill Forsyth*

Kawasaki almost tasted victory in 500cc GP motocross in 1980, when Brad Lackey narrowly missed taking the world title. Two years later, and restricted by its own modest resources, Kawasaki's motocross goals still had not been realized, with British rider Dave Thorpe placing sixth in the 1982 World Championship with an air-cooled KX500.

Kawasaki's motocross focus shifted to the U.S.A. in 1983, competing across all three AMA capacity categories with respective water-cooled SR125s and SR250s and a new SR500.

The 1983 SR500 was Kawasaki's first water-cooled works 500. A clear indication of the technology it represented is that it was built in late 1982, a full three years before Kawasaki released its first production water-cooled KX500. The 1985 production model KX500 was based on this exact bike.

Even though the evolution model SR500s that followed during the mid-1980s could at best only repeat Lackey's second place in a World Championship, the SR's role as a template for subsequent KX production models helped fast-track GP motocross technology to weekend Kawasaki racers.

Kent Howerton's 1983 SR500
This 1983 SR500 is one of four made by Kawasaki Heavy Industries' Motorcycle Racing Division and was used by Texas rider Kent Howerton to campaign all rounds of the

The "low boy" tank design introduced in 1985 was retained in 1986. The SR500 never made it to the top of the World 500 Championship points table. *Bill Forsyth*

Kent Howerton played a vital role in developing the 1983 SR500. Even the hand-formed exhaust pipes were changed according to track conditions. *Bill Forsyth*

U.S. National Championship as well as the American round of the World 500 GP, held in California. Howerton won three rounds of the U.S. National 500 Championship on this bike in 1983 but was overtaken in the second half of the season by Yamaha's Broc Glover on a works OW500. Other identical SR500s were ridden in England by Kurt Nicoll and Dave Watson.

Kent Howerton had been poached away from Suzuki to ride for Kawasaki in 1983, and his role was made clear right from the start. He was expected to win races and also to be intimately involved in the development of all of Kawasaki's works bikes. Constant changes were made to the bikes Howerton raced, resulting in technology that often found its way onto Kawasaki production models within a year or two. Kawasaki gave Howerton a free hand to improve whatever was necessary. His input was particularly relevant, as Howerton

had come to Kawasaki from Suzuki. Suzuki had just developed the Full Floater suspension, which was far superior to the Kawasaki Uni-Trak system.

Kent recalls, "Compared to other works bikes, Kawasaki used more production parts. This bike was not really any different from any other Kawasaki works bikes of the day. The engine was basically a stock bottom end that had been modified to accept a water-cooled top end. As far as the power the bike made, it was very smooth and very fast. Suspension was the weak link—it needed a lot of attention and just didn't work all that good."

At the U.S. Grand Prix at Carlsbad, California, Kent placed the SR500 in sixth, riding against the fastest 500-class riders in the world. Later that same year, Kawasaki flew the bike to Europe, where Jeff Ward rode it in the Motocross des Nations. The American team won for the third year in a row.

The year 1984 had the potential to be one of the toughest seasons ever in 500 GP motocross. Yamaha was buoyed by Hakan Carlqvist's 1983 World Championship win, and Honda set its sights on the crown with one of its most talented rider lineups ever: Andre Malherbe, Eric Geboers, Dave Thorpe, and Andre Vromans, under the management of American Steve Whitelock. Even though reigning 500cc champion Carlqvist was still riding an air-cooled Yamaha, his biggest handicap was a pre-season injury that was destined to impede the hard-charging Swede.

Against this backdrop, the 1983 World 250cc champion, Belgian Georges Jobe, had made the switch from Suzuki to Kawasaki. His arrival marked a bolder international motocross commitment by Kawasaki, and Jobe faced off against the new Honda RC500s of Malherbe and Geboers. Dave Thorpe and Andre Vromans stayed with '83 model Hondas that were updated with new components. While nothing would stop the Honda RC500s that went on to dominate 500cc motocross during 1984 and 1985, Jobe's SR500 Kawasaki finished second, splitting Honda's new champion, Andre Malherbe, and Dave Thorpe in the process.

The 1983 model SR500 was Kawasaki's first water-cooled 500cc works bike. It appeared three years before the production-model KX500 of 1985. *Bill Forsyth*

Georges Jobe's 1984 SR500 was Kawasaki's second water-cooled 500 GP racer, and its execution was a major step up from the 1983 model. Jobe's first season opened brilliantly. He was immediately successful on the new SR, winning the first two GP rounds in Austria and Switzerland. He also went on to win the Canadian GP and finish second in Sweden and third in England, but mechanical problems in Spain and France cost him dearly. In addition, he injured his foot, stretching some ligaments just before the West German GP, and was forced to compete in the next few races wearing a cast.

Throughout the German, Dutch, and American GPs, Jobe saw his championship hopes fading, as he was unable to perform at his best. Nevertheless, he made a comeback in the last five events, beating eventual 1984 champion Andre Malherbe in every race but one moto in Belgium.

Despite these problems, Jobe finished second in the World Championship to Malherbe by just 10 points. Obviously pleased with his performance and the potential of the SR500, Jobe went on to sign with Kawasaki for two more years, 1985 and 1986.

Georges Jobe's 1984 SR500

The 1984 SR500 was the lightest 500 on the GP circuit, weighing in at 225 pounds—16.5 pounds lighter than Kawasaki's 1983 works bike. With sand-cast magnesium hubs, a large-capacity aluminum fuel tank, and a hand-made frame, the SR's detailing was impressive. Styling was based on the KX125, making the SR appear and feel as small as possible.

Kawasaki's 1984 swingarm was fabricated along the same lines as the works Honda RC500s, moving away

from the box-section style of 1983. Attempts had also been made to bring the riding position forward and to lower the center of gravity by reshaping the fuel tank. Its increased capacity was to overcome the embarrassment of running out of fuel that occurred on the 1983 SR500 in longer motos.

Suspension refinements included handmade 43mm billet forks with adjustable damping and teflon-coated seals. Hand-machined and -welded triple clamps were available in a variety of offsets to alter handling characteristics. A gullwing-style lower triple clamp offered exceptional rigidity and allowed the forks more travel while at

the same time reducing fork underhang for better clearance through ruts.

The rear shock had an inbuilt heat compensator to reduce damper fade during longer races and was also a billet item, with adjustable rebound and two-stage compression damping. Also new for 1984 was ride-height adjustment by a new Uni-Trak link.

Although overshadowed by Honda's domination of the 500cc Championship, Jobe's 1984 SR500 paved the way for Kawasaki's first production water-cooled KX500, the 1985 model KX500B1. The KX proved to be a sales success for Kawasaki and shared styling and chassis geometry with the 1984 SR500, as well as its plastics, which became production items for 1985.

Georges Jobe's 1985 SR500

In 1985, Honda was destined to make it two in a row in international 500cc motocross, with Thorpe and Malherbe jointly winning 23 out of 24 motos throughout the season on the invincible RC500s. Suzuki's timely departure from the class in 1984 might have provided some added incentive for Kawasaki to topple Honda's "Red Team," as Jobe referred to them, but the 1985 SR500 failed to make motocross history. Jobe could manage no better than fourth place by the end of the season, and the SR500 went largely ignored, as the motorcycle press focussed on Honda's flawless duo, Dave Thorpe and Andrew Malherbe.

Fourth place for Jobe was little compensation for himself or Kawasaki, and much of the 1985 SR's innovative engineering went unnoticed, including Kawasaki's move to a rear disc brake, its reservoir mounted outboard of the right-side frame rails. It was also Kawasaki's first works 500 to be fitted with a power valve in an effort to smooth and manage the water-cooled 500's awesome output. This could be adjusted for individual circuit conditions by means of a spring-loaded governor and became a production KX component in 1986.

Kawasaki's technology and resulting components also continued in the '85 SR plastics, which went on to become 1986 production parts. Other SR parts remained strictly one-off, marking the works Kawasakis as hand-built, single-purpose racers, sophisticated within their own sphere of competition as the best multicylinder road racers.

For 1985, an aluminum "low boy" tank dropped the center of gravity even further than previously, and the forks featured billet-machined lower sections with an ingenious fold-out clamp to secure the axle. Its purpose was to speed up trackside wheel changes in the event of a puncture. Kawasaki also made the SR clutch cover in two sections so that the clutch could be replaced without removing the entire side cover—a lightweight piece roughly sand cast in magnesium.

Kawasaki's sole official factory racing commitment throughout 1985 had been motocross, yet the company was still well short of its goals. Fortunes did not change in 1986, when Jobe wound up his season with yet another fourth spot. Development of the SR500 continued throughout 1987, but even Kurt Nicoll could do no better for Kawasaki than to equal Lackey's long-forgotten second place that year and again in 1988. The SR500 was abandoned in 1989 and never reached development with a perimeter frame.

No Kawasaki SR500 rider made it to the top spot of a World 500 Motocross Championship points table. Even after a decade of development, the bike that had given Kawasaki so much valuable techno feedback for its production motocrossers would be remembered only as a steppingstone.

The 1985 SR500 used Teflon-coated fork seals and microfinished fork tubes to reduce stiction. The triple clamps were made of billet sections welded together for strength. Uni-Trak ride height was adjustable.
Bill Forsyth

Jeff Ward's 1985 SR250 and 1992 KX250

Jeff Ward's First and Last 250 Kawasakis

The 1985 SR250 frame was hand built, as was the thin-wall aluminum fuel tank. *Bill Forsyth*

Jeff Ward's transition from mini cycle champion to Indy car racer spanned more than 20 years. During that period, his name was synonymous with Kawasaki's motocross presence in the U.S.A. and also as seven-time representative for his country in the prestigious annual Motocross des Nations. Jeff was part of the winning U.S.A. team on five occasions.

Born in Scotland, Jeff Ward moved with his family to the west coast of the U.S. in the early 1960s and started racing at age four. As a prelude to the motocross career that followed, Jeff was a cameo star in the Bruce Brown film *On Any Sunday*, the then five-year-old kid popping wheelies on a Honda QA50 mini bike. His talent was apparent even then. By 1975, Jeff was sponsored by Honda, racing and winning on a highly modified XR75 and featuring prominently in Honda's U.S. advertising for its new four-stroke mini racer.

Jeff Ward turned pro racer in 1978, forging a relationship with Kawasaki that was to endure for 14 years—his entire motocross career. His first National 125cc win for Kawasaki came in 1982, at age 21, and by 1984, Jeff's SR125 dominated the capacity class, earning him his first U.S. National Championship title. Jeff still rates his 1984 works SR125 as the best 125cc motocross machine ever produced.

One of Ward's two 1984 SR125s now sits in Greg Primm's personal motocross museum, The Primm Collection,

Jeff Ward's 1985 SR250 marked Kawasaki's final year with exotic factory one-offs and won both AMA 250 Motocross and Supercross titles. *Bill Forsyth*

Even though Mike Kiedrowski won the outdoor AMA 500 National Championships for Kawasaki in 1992, it was not a high-profile year for Jeff Ward or his KX250. *Bill Forsyth*

in Las Vegas, Nevada, along with Jeff's 1975 Honda XR75. The other SR125 is part of a collection of factory race bikes preserved by Kawasaki Motors Corporation U.S.A. in Irvine, California.

In 1985, Ward moved away from his much-loved SR125 up to the 250cc class, taking out both the AMA 250 Motocross and Supercross titles in his debut year on the SR250. While this was Ward's first year with the works SR250, with its handmade frame and swingarm and lightweight aluminum fuel tank, it was also the final season for the exotic factory specials. The year 1986 saw the introduction of more production-based AMA rules that effectively outlawed all one-off works machines.

Jeff Ward's 1985 SR250 is also part of Kawasaki's collection in Irvine. The final evolution of a motocross bloodline that began in 1972 with the custom C&J-framed Kawasakis of Brad Lackey, this bike weighed very close to the 216-pound AMA weight limit.

In common with Kawasaki's 1985 production KX models, the SR's five-speed motor used the new KIPS

power valve system, which slowly opened the exhaust ports as engine rpm increased, giving smoother roll-on power, along with improved traction and response. It also used FAIS, the new fresh air intake system introduced that year, and paved the way for further developments of the production KX250D2 in 1986, such as a higher compression ratio, a larger 40mm Mikuni carb, and a boost in power to 48 horsepower at 8,000 rpm.

At the track, Ward was renowned for his deep concentration and focus rather than any ability to beam smiles on cue. In 1987, he won his second Supercross title for Kawasaki, followed by a second Outdoor National 250 Championship in 1988. Throughout his career, Ward scored 50 Outdoor National and 20 Supercross victories and won at least one Supercross event per year from 1984 to 1991. When he topped this up with 500-class National Championship wins in 1989 and 1990, beating Honda's Jeff Stanton, he became the first American rider to win titles in every class of motocross.

After the factory had endured two mediocre years in European GP motocross, Ward's 500-class U.S. wins could not have been better timed for Kawasaki. The gods also favored green in the 125cc class that year, with Mike Kiedrowski taking his first AMA title before going on to win the AMA 500 Championship in 1992. Kawasaki's Mike LaRocco kept the pressure up the following year with another AMA 500 Championship win.

Fourteen years after signing with Kawasaki, Jeff Ward made the decision to move into four-wheel motorsports, setting his sights on Indy cars and a transition through the Indy Racing Light support class ranks. His final year in motocross was 1992. He rode his last Kawasaki, a production-based KX250, in both Supercross and outdoor events.

Like all other U.S. Team Kawasaki bikes of the period, Ward's last KX was prepared in California and started life as a stock production KX250. Modifications included factory Kyaba suspension, some engine development, and the use of T8 titanium nuts and bolts to help trim the weight down to just 2 pounds above the AMA's 216-pound limit.

The 1992 production-based KX250 was Jeff Ward's last race bike before moving to auto racing in Indy Racing Lights. *Bill Forsyth*

While '92 was not Jeff Ward's winningest year in either motocross or Supercross, he remained a firm favorite with his loyal legions of fans and rode the KX250 in parade laps after each event. After he retired at the end of the '92 season, Jeff was voted Motocrosser of the Decade by *Dirt Rider* magazine, which also quoted him as saying, "Motocross is a physical sport . . . car racing is a technological sport."

His prophetic observations proved true. When Jeff started car racing, it took the gritty rookie three years in the Indy Light support classes to pay his dues before his debut Indy car drive in 1995. Unfortunately, a number of mechanical problems forced him to miss the last moments of the essential qualifying session at the Indianapolis Brickyard that year, and the ex-motocross multichampion saw his dream fade. Ward had hoped to be the first motocrosser to race and win the Indy 500.

This dream has yet to be realized, but that has not lessened Jeff Ward's resolve. He went on to be nominated Rookie of the Year at Indianapolis and has also scored second-, third-, and fourth-place finishes. In mid-2002, shortly after signing with Chip Ganassi Racing, he won his first race, the Boomtown 500 at Texas Motor Speedway, in a photo finish with Al Unser.

Some uncertainty clouds the credentials of the bike believed to be Jeff Ward's last Kawasaki—the 1992-season KX250. This bike has been totally restored by a well-known California motocross specialist and is faithful to Jeff Ward's specifications, right down to an original seat cover the owner sourced as a spare from the original supplier. Whether this actual bike is Jeff Ward's last ride may be impossible to prove or disprove, but that does not weaken the claim Jeff Ward and Kawasaki jointly staked out on American motocross for almost one and a half decades.

PART 4

The 1990s and Beyond

2001 Yamaha YZ250F

Getting Up to Light Speed

When Yamaha announced the YZ400F four-stroke in 1997, the global impact on motocross was instant and predictable. With the first production YZ400F models scheduled for 1998, the motocross market went into an immediate holding pattern as Yamaha milked the publicity benefits of its new 317-pound thumper.

With its 92mm x 60.1mm short-stroke DOHC engine echoing the configuration of the Swedish Husaberg, the YZF weighed just 22 pounds more than the two-stroke YZ250 Yamaha's engineers had used as a performance yardstick. Five valves and an 11,000 rpm performance ceiling set new parameters for a Japanese manufacturer, taking Yamaha into the big–four-stroke territory traditionally held by the race-oriented Euro brands: Husaberg, KTM, and Husqvarna.

After the initial love affair with the YZ400F cooled marginally, criticism began to emerge. Yamaha was quick to respond with an upgraded 2000 model YZ426F. As well as the obvious increase in engine capacity, thanks to a larger, 95mm bore, Yamaha also upspec'd the YZF con rod, crankshaft, carb, CDI ignition, hot-start system, exhaust, radiators, clutch plates, gear ratios, and suspension. The result was a smoother powerband, with buckets of power from just off idle to peak rpm.

For average riders, the 426 was more user-friendly, with less of the hard-hitting, brutal power that characterized the YZ400F and had endeared it to Pro-level racers.

The aftermarket was quick to respond with a massive inventory of horsepower and weight-reduction modifications for the YZ250F. *Bill Forsyth*

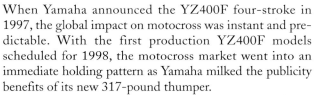

Design inspiration for the YZ250F came directly from Yamaha's YZ400F and YZ426F and the YZ125 two-stroke. *Bill Forsyth*

The YZ250F was the first production 250cc four-stroke motocrosser from any manufacturer, European or Japanese. *Bill Forsyth*

For the top guns, the new 426 was an even better platform for an aftermarket modified race-winning package.

There was no doubt that both the 400 and 426 grabbed the attention they deserved. In just two years, Yamaha had reinvented itself as the company capable of dominating motocross with both two-stroke and four-stroke designs. While other Japanese manufacturers previewed concepts, Yamaha took its to production. Already into its second generation, its 500cc class four-stroke faced no immediate threat from Suzuki, Honda, or Kawasaki.

It would have been easy for the company to sit on its laurels, but Yamaha took the successful YZF concept one step further with the announcement of the YZ250F in mid-2000. Once again Yamaha had shifted the goalposts. Here was the first production 250cc four-stroke motocross machine for any manufacturer, European or Japanese. The debut of the YZ250F not only reaffirmed Yamaha's commitment to an increased four-stroke component of its dirt bike inventory but also upped the stakes for any other company aspiring to follow suit.

Inspiration for the YZ250F did not come from any other noncompetition four-stroke but directly from the YZ400/426 and Yamaha's own YZ125 two-stroke. The new bike used a YZ125 chassis as the starting point for its own development, mated to a scaled-down dry-sump, liquid-cooled, five-valve DOHC engine that was virtually indistinguishable from the larger 400 and 426 powerplants. Standard equipment even included titanium valves.

Yamaha turned up the throttle on its publicity machine, capitalizing on Doug Dubach's involvement in the YZ250F development program. Early feedback from other Yamaha "A Listers," such as Craig Dack and Chad Reed, also backed up pitside patter that the YZ250F was about to change the face of the dirt bike market. Craig Dack, then manager of the Australian-based Team CDR Yamaha prior to his move to the U.S.A., said after returning from test sessions in California, "I was blown away with the thing. . . . It's got a beautiful power delivery and seems to steer even better than a 125 motocrosser."

Chad Reed was equally impressed, adding, "It's got to be the most user-friendly dirt bike I've ever ridden, and like the 426, it's fully capable of doing everything a two-stroke motocrosser does."

Short of walking on water, the YZ250F seemed almost capable of miracles, with the bulk of motorcycle magazine testers concluding that the 250F delivered a punch that combined four-stroke spread and torque and fast-revving, responsive, two-stroke power characteristics.

Out in the aftermarket, both the 400 and 426 had already spawned their own network of equipment suppliers, all capable of helping would-be YZ buyers to divest themselves of unwanted cash. In time-honored fashion, the YZ250F maintained the tradition. YZ owners were swamped by a relentless wave of modifications capable of delivering up to an extra 10 horsepower, along with weight reduction to the tune of 11 pounds or more. At the time when a standard YZ250F cost around $5,500, a typical aftermarket shopping list could add as much as $7,500 to that price.

The innovative Yamaha Race of Champions at Glen Helen faced off great riders of the past on a range of current-model YZs. The four-stroke YZ250F was Stephen Gall's favorite. *Mitch Friedman, YROC 2002*

Modified YZ250Fs, such as the $15,000 example created by Mike Tolle Racing of Riverside, California, endorsed the YZF with even greater credibility at the very top of the motocross subculture. Mike is no newcomer to motocross R&D and worked with Chaparral as well as on the U.S. national race circuit before setting up his own shop to cater to customers' motocross fantasies.

Mike prefers to keep his YZs internally stock so that he can stick with standard pump fuel and retain maximum reliability. Instead of internal magic, he draws on lightweight, bolt-on componentry and external mods that broaden the powerband as well as boost maximum output. The result is power with a seamless bottom-end to midrange transition, which Mike describes as "mellow and forgiving . . . and better than a stock YZ426F."

Bolstered by six years of opposition inactivity in the four-stroke motocross market, Yamaha will enter 2004 to face Honda's growing CRF four-stroke motocross lineup in both 450cc and 250cc variants. If Yamaha's most recent history is to repeat itself, who knows what fresh technology might be unveiled?

2002 Honda CRF450R

Prince of Progress

The SOHC liquid-cooled Honda Unicam four-valve is 449cc and weighs 65 pounds. *Bill Forsyth*

Honda Motor Company's founder, Soichiro Honda, was absolutely committed to achieving leadership in technology. As early as 1954, just six years after its establishment, Honda Motor Company faced possible bankruptcy, but Soichiro Honda countered any rumors by issuing a bold proclamation. It left his dedication to winning in motorcycle sports and lifting the standards of Japanese industry in little doubt: "I have decided to participate in the TT race next year. This aim is definitely a difficult one, but we have to achieve it to test the viability of Japanese industrial technology and demonstrate it to the world. Our mission is the enlightenment of Japanese industry."

However, Honda's relationship with the sport of motocross has long been marked by paradox. The same manufacturer that showed the way with the revolutionary Honda Elsinore CR250M in 1973 also fell by the wayside within two years with outmoded subsequent 125cc and 250cc production models.

Soichiro Honda's personal passion for small-capacity, four-stroke racing engines was as legendary as his indifference to two-strokes, yet the company he founded was slow to combine its four-stroke expertise and motocross ambitions. Even the success of Honda's XL and XR off-road models did little to stimulate Honda as the growing shift toward four-stroke motocross machines gathered momentum in the late 1990s. Honda remained seemingly oblivious to this trend.

32

The CRF450R is also Honda's first production four-stroke motocrosser. *Bill Forsyth*

On the sales floor and on racetracks around the world, Honda's alloy perimeter-framed two-stroke CRs were holding their own. They continued to showcase the company's leading-edge motocross technology, so Honda resisted the temptation to enter the four-stroke marketplace with any new model that might be compromised through hasty execution.

Honda may have been patient, but not so the motocross market. Yamaha seized the moment with the launch of the YZ400F four-stroke in 1998, followed by the headline-grabbing YZ250F less than three years later. Their arrival not only scored kudos for Yamaha but also stimulated a broad acceptance of four-stroke motocrossers as the inevitable shape of the future.

The conservatism Honda had shown by staying on the sidelines for three years was not rewarded until 2002, with the launch of the CRF450R—the world's only alloy perimeter-framed, four-stroke motocrosser. It was also Honda's first production four-stroke motocrosser, and its debut coincided perfectly with a market that was becoming a little jaded by endless seas of blue or orange four-strokes.

Magazines were quick to line up the CRF450R in comparative shootouts between the YZ426F and later the YZ450F Yamaha. Most reports concluded there was little to differentiate between the two brands, with the lighter Honda taking the honors for its overall excellent rideability over the snappier YZF. Not even the KTM 520SX could equal Honda's "zero hesitation" engine response.

Blatant technology helped Honda move to the high ground that Yamaha once held exclusively. The debut of the CRF450R saw Honda sharing techno bragging rights with its rival, a position Honda was happy to sustain by unfolding the mouthwatering specs of the new red racer.

After some initial concerns in the marketplace, Honda's twin-spar alloy frame was now in its third generation. Motocross riders had finally accepted the company line that Honda used the enveloping alloy frame for strength rather than weight saving. Based on the 2002 CR250R chassis and weighing just half a pound more, it allowed the use of larger, more rigid structures than would ever be possible in steel and provided the perfect chassis package for a motor that would once again raise the standards of four-stroke technology. Almost 50 years later, Soichiro Honda's words had not been forgotten.

The compact Honda liquid-cooled, four-valve, SOHC 449cc Unicam engine weighed 65 pounds, almost identical to the marginally heavier YZ and KTM powerplants. With a highly oversquare short-stroke design and titanium inlet valves, the CRF450R developed peak power at 7,500 rpm—exactly midway between the 9,000 rpm ceiling of the YZ and the conservative 7,500 rpm KTM.

Inside lurked a forged two-ring piston that looked like a 96mm alloy pancake—just 1.5 inches tall, almost devoid of a skirt, and protected by a ceramic coating on both the piston crown and skirt areas. At just 267 grams, the CRF piston was only 70 percent the weight of a conventional, fully skirted design. Additional weight savings were achieved through the use of a Nicasil-plated cylinder, a titanium exhaust header, and a rebuildable aluminum-bodied muffler.

Honda engineers separated the lubrication needs of engine and transmission, using two individual systems. By separating engine and transmission oils, they eliminated any chances of clutch-contaminated transmission oil reaching the engine lubrication system. The five-speed transmission needed no pump, which in turn allowed for a smaller, lighter engine-oil pump, using less power.

In just five years, the rules of four-stroke motocross warfare had been radically revamped—first by Yamaha, then by Honda, with a single motorcycle that graphically demonstrated just how far technology had progressed in a sport that was itself only 50 years old. Comparing Honda's 2003 CRF450R to BSA's then state-of-the-art 1965 BSA 441 Victor GP drives this point home even more dramatically.

The 96mm CRF450R engine bore is actually larger than the 90mm stroke of the old BSA B44 engine, with the Honda delivering around 55 horsepower at 9,000 rpm. That's 66 percent more power than that of the BSA and at 50 percent higher engine rpm. On the scales, the CRF topped out at 225 pounds, compared to

Fifty-four years after its founding, Honda launched the world's only alloy perimeter-framed, four-stroke motocrosser—the CRF450R.
Bill Forsyth

the more compact 441 Victor at 255 pounds. While the late seventies are often touted as the Golden Age of motocross technology because of the rapid advances in suspension systems, the CRF450R makes a strong case in favor of the opening years of the current millennium. The age of the four-stroke has finally arrived.

The entry and immediate acceptance of the CRF450R in the world of motocross have defined a new timeline for the sport. For Honda, its timing has been flawless.

By the end of 2002, there was no doubt that Honda's biggest motocross coup had been to lure former Kawasaki star Ricky Carmichael to Ride Red. Carmichael proceeded to pay back his new employer with an astounding

11 out of 16 race wins in the 2002 AMA Supercross Championship, followed by absolute domination of the U.S. 250 National Motocross Championship. By the end of the 2002 season, Carmichael had won every moto in which he competed—24 in a row.

So will the CRF450R prove to be Honda's next great motocross milestone? The massive response by the aftermarket industry already indicates that the Honda will be as extensively supported as both the YZ250 and YZ400/426/450F Yamahas. And Honda has even more up its sleeve, with the announcement of a new 250-class four-stroke based on the CRF450R. The CRF250R is scheduled for the 2004 racing season.

2003 KTM 525SX

Orange Appeal

A factory 540SXS kit transforms the production 2003 KTM 525SX into a mainstream market GP replica. *Bill Forsyth*

Fifty years ago, the first of three R100 motorcycles to carry the KTM tank badge rolled off the modest assembly line at the Trunkenpolz family-owned factory in Mattighofen, Austria. The small automotive repair shop founded by Hans Trunkenpolz in 1934 had expanded into motorcycle manufacturing, and its staff of 20 was capable of producing three KTM R100s each day. Just three years later, KTM made its mark in ISDT competition. A gold-medal win by Egon Dornauer's KTM125 in the 1956 event hinted at KTM's longer-term ambitions of creating a range of specialized, lightweight, off-road motorcycles.

By 1968, KTM was producing 1,000 motorcycles per year and had opened up the U.S. market via John Penton, an entrepreneurial enduro rider from Ohio, who approached the Austrian factory to build export KTM models to his own specifications. Badged as Pentons for sale in the U.S.A., these lightweight 125cc and 175cc KTM models redefined America's concept of what constitutes a great dirt bike. By contrast to the heavier, larger-engined machines of the day, the KTM/Pentons were light, responsive, and also nearly indestructible.

By 1974, Kraftfahrzeuge Trunkenpolz Mattighofen (KTM) was manufacturing 42 different motorcycle and scooter models. That year also marked KTM's first World 250cc Motocross Championship title win by Russian rider Gennady Moiseev. Two years later, during which the 250 class was dominated by Belgium's Harry Everts and

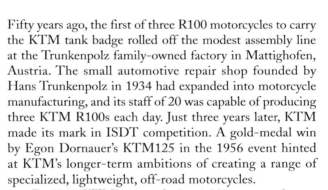

After a five-year development program, KTM introduced its own SOHC 560cc motor in 1987. Current-generation race motors were announced in 1999. *Bill Forsyth*

33

Finnish rider Heikki Mikkola, Moiseev regained the 250 crown for KTM in 1977 and 1978.

Motocross was high on the KTM corporate agenda by the early eighties. Austria's Heinz Kinigadner took the 250cc World title in 1984 and followed up, Moiseev-style, in 1985 with a second KTM victory. In 1989, KTM's motocross domination flowed over into the 125cc category when American rider Trampas Parker won KTM's first 125-class World Championship title. At the same time, Broc Glover was competing in European 250 GPs, riding a prototype that would reach production the following year as 250cc and 300cc replicas.

KTM had always been innovative. It followed up the 1982 launching of its s own single-shock, linkage-rear-suspension "Pro Lever" bikes by becoming, in 1986, the first off-road motorcycle manufacturer to fit front and rear disc brakes as standard equipment. Then, after a five-year development program for the first liquid-cooled four-stroke single, KTM introduced its own SOHC 560cc motor in 1987, at a time when production in Austria and at the Lorain, Ohio, plant of KTM America Inc. totaled 10,000 motorcycles.

KTM remained privately owned by the founding Trunkenpolz family until 1989, when it was taken over that year by GIT Trust Holding, an investment group.

The combination turned sour after GIT tried to diversify beyond the core motorcycle product into unrelated markets.

In 1991, KTM filed for bankruptcy in Austria but emerged the following year under new management as KTM Sportmotorcycle Gmbh. A further renaming as KTM Sportmotorcycle AG followed in 1994. What emerged was a stronger and more focused organization, backed by new owners with a vision and passion for a definitive breed of dirt bike. New capital and fresh thinking escalated a process of refinement and development that had started in the early nineties.

When KTM went orange in 1996, the results were obvious—new-look motorcycles with bold, aggressive character. The makeover coincided perfectly with KTM's first 500cc World Championship title. This time, the honors went to a New Zealand rider—Shayne King.

By 1999, KTM had unveiled its new-generation competition four-strokes, strict racing engines in both 400cc and 520cc variants. Even though these machines would take until the following year to reach the marketplace, their introduction paved the way for Belgium's Joel Smets to stamp his move to KTM from Husaberg with a 500-class World Championship win.

What KTM put into production for 2000 with the 520SX was precisely the same formula Yamaha had applied to the creation of the YZ400F two years previously: a completely new-generation engine wrapped in a no-compromise, two-stroke–style frame. The simpler but more powerful four-valve, wet-sump SOHC KTM engine was at no disadvantage to the YZ. It produced power everywhere it was needed—but more important, its torque delivery from 3,000 to 6,000 rpm was unmatched by anything else, so a four-speed gearbox was all the KTM required. The 520's broad power spread and heavy-flywheel feel quickly endeared it to riders who were confident with its more "traditional four-stroke" manners.

Detail changes, including slimmer ergonomics on the 2001 520SX model, widened the appeal of a race bike that was less demanding than even the improved YZ426F but that still gave away nothing on the race track.

Not even the appearance of Honda's CRF450R in 2002 diminished the KTM 520's status. With an actual dry weight of 243 pounds, the 525SX was about 5 pounds lighter than the YZ but some 10 pounds heavier than a CRF450R Honda. Somehow, the KTM's slim lines and minimalist styling still impressed, and countless test comparisons yielded similar results. They said that the KTM simply "felt smaller and lighter," and its appeal embraced riders from Pro-class experts down to moderately talented weekend racers.

Sophisticated brand marketing then took this perception one stage further. KTM raised the bar one notch higher with its introduction of SXS Factory Parts—a comprehensive and integrated range of race components which could transform any production KTM SX into a veritable factory replica. This level of sophistication did not come cheap, but that only enhanced the appeal and mystique of SXS Factory Parts. KTM's SXS Factory Parts catalog tempted with goodies that included 48mm WP upside-down forks with matching triple clamps, optional wheel assemblies, big-bore conversions, featherweight titanium exhaust systems, and a host of carbon-fiber accessories.

Innovative engineering is only a single element behind the success of KTM's 520/525 series racers. With a strong focus on rider and product support, KTM has seemingly turned back the motocross clock to an earlier time, when brand loyalty meant more than cutting a deal at the local bike shop. Marketing experts call it "added value." Few motocross racers would disagree, particularly when their KTM525SX delivers its weekly dose of adrenaline and ear-to-ear grins.

The powerful, four-valve, wet-sump SOHC KTM engine produces power across a broad range. Torque delivery from 3,000 to 6,000 rpm is unmatched, so only a four-speed gearbox is required.
Bill Forsyth

Index

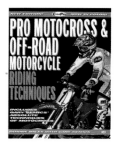

**Pro Motocross and Off-Road
Riding Techniques**
ISBN 0-7603-0831-4

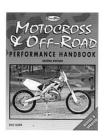

**Motocross and Off-Road
Performance Handbook**
ISBN 0-7603-0660-5

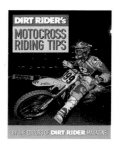

**Dirt Rider's
Motorcross Riding tips**
ISBN 0-7603-1315-6

**Freestyle Motocross:
Jump Tricks From the Pros**
ISBN 0-7603-0926-4

**Freestyle Motocross II:
Air Sickness**
ISBN 0-7603-1184-6

Streetbike Extreme
ISBN 0-7603-1299-0

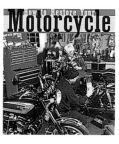

**How To Restore
Your Motorcycle**
ISBN 0-7603-0681-8

**Leanings: The Best of Peter
Egan from Cycle World**
ISBN 0-7603-1158-7